WONDERS OF MAN

TOWER OF LONDON

by Christopher Hibbert

and the Editors
of the Newsweek Book Division

Published in the United Kingdom by

The Reader's Digest Association Limited, London

in association with

NEWSWEEK, New York

NEWSWEEK BOOK DIVISION

JOSEPH L. GARDNER   *Editor*

Edwin D. Bayrd, Jr.   *Associate Editor*
Laurie P. Phillips   *Picture Editor*
Eva Galan   *Assistant Editor*
Lynne H. Brown   *Copy Editor*
Russell Ash   *European Correspondent*

Alvin Garfin   *Publisher*

WONDERS OF MAN

MILTON GENDEL   *Consulting Editor*

Contents

Introduction

To the hundreds of thousands who visit it each year, the Tower of London excites grisly visions of imprisonment, torture, and violent death. "In truth there is no sadder spot on the earth," wrote the nineteenth-century English historian Thomas Babington Macaulay. "Thither have been carried, through successive ages, by the rude hands of gaolers, without one mourner following, the bleeding relics of men who had been the captains of armies, the leaders of parties, the oracles of senates, and the ornaments of courts."

There is much more than violence to the Tower's story, of course, and the author of the following lively narrative uses the awesome citadel as a stage for a panoramic sweep through nine hundred years of English history. Few battles have been more decisive than the one fought at Hastings in October 1066, for the Norman victors brought to Saxon England a new dynasty, a new nobility, a new culture, and the seeds of a new language. Following his historic triumph, William the Conqueror erected a series of fortresses to protect his newly won island kingdom—the most imposing of which was the White Tower, heart of the present Tower of London complex.

For centuries before it became the prison that has given it such a fearsome reputation, the Tower was a richly ornamented medieval palace and a nearly impregnable royal fortress. With the advent of the notorious Henry VIII, it became the dread destination of the ruler's enemies—and the site of numerous executions. As Queen Elizabeth I undoubtedly knew when she was brought to the Tower as a princess in bondage, entering through its Thames-side Traitor's Gate was often the first step to the execution block. Happily, Elizabeth I emerged from the Tower unscathed. A number of her opponents and rivals were less lucky: they lost their heads there at her command.

Elizabeth's Stuart successors greatly expanded the royal mint, the menagerie for exotic beasts, and the museum, which already were housed at the Tower. Although prisoners were held there as recently as World War II, public beheadings on nearby Tower Hill ceased in 1747. But the museum, with its splendid collection of armor and its fabulous display of the incomparable crown jewels, continues to be one of England's most popular tourist attractions.

THE EDITORS

THE STORY
OF THE
TOWER OF LONDON

I

A CASTLE FOR THE CONQUEROR

High in the dark skies above Western Europe that winter there shone a comet, sure portent of disaster.

In England, King Edward, great-great-great-grandson of Alfred the Great, lay dying in his riverside palace outside London's western gate. Beyond the windows of his bedchamber rose the towering stone walls of the new abbey that his masons had begun building fifteen years earlier. The work was almost finished now. Plans had been made for the consecration of the church on December 28, Innocents' Day, when his wife, Queen Edith, would take his place at the splendid ceremony. And — as though he had been waiting only for that day to take his leave of life — as soon as he learned that the service had been conducted satisfactorily, he prepared himself for death.

Yet King Edward could not die in peace. True, the great task of building Westminster Abbey, to which he had devoted so much thought and prayer and money during the last pious years of his life, was successfully accomplished. But the import of that comet, glaringly illuminating the night sky above his deathbed, could not be ignored. A crisis was at hand. Recovering the power of speech, which he had temporarily lost, the king prophesied that a time of evil was coming over the land. With that prediction he died. The date was January 5, 1066.

King Edward — known to history as Edward the Confessor — died childless, and the crown of England was at stake. Four powerful men immediately laid claim to it. Two of them were brothers of the queen: Tostig, Earl of Northumbria until 1065, and Harold Godwinson, Earl of Wessex. A third claimant was Harold III Haardraade, King of Norway. The fourth was William, Duke of Normandy, whose claim was genealogically the strongest since both he and Edward were directly descended from a former Duke of Normandy, Richard I.

Ignoring his Norman cousin's claim, Edward, when dying, had nominated his brother-in-law Harold as his successor. And Harold, making immediate use of this advantage over his rivals, had had himself crowned king in the new abbey of Westminster on the very day that its founder was buried there.

Such speed was essential, for it was already known that both King Harold's brother, Tostig, then living in exile in Flanders, and Haardraade, King of Norway, were preparing to invade England. Tostig's forces landed first, harrying the Isle of Wight at the beginning of May, invading Kent, and then sailing up the east coast to pour ashore at Lincolnshire. Defeated by local levies, Tostig retreated north to await the arrival of Haardraade, whom he now intended to support.

Four months later the three hundred ships of King Haardraade's army appeared off the northeastern coast of England. Joined by Tostig's men, the Scandinavian warriors sailed up the Humber, scrambled ashore at Riccall, and then marched on York where they defeated the levies of Morcar, who had replaced Tostig as Earl of Northumbria.

King Harold, who was in the south preparing to withstand a third invasion — the threatened attack from Normandy — marched north immediately. He overwhelmed his enemies in a brilliant victory at Stamford Bridge, during the course of which both Tostig and Haardraade were killed. But while Harold's exhausted troops were resting at York, a change of wind in the Channel enabled Duke William to cross from Normandy and disembark his knights on the English coast at Pevensey.

Bringing his troops south again with all possible speed, Harold arrived in London on October 6. Five days later, having collected all the reinforcements he could muster under his banner, he marched south for the Sussex Downs, where he hoped to take William by surprise and to cut him off from his ships, which lay at anchor at Hastings. As it happened, it was Harold who was caught by surprise. Riding out of Hastings early on the morning of October 14, William and his knights came in sight of Harold's infantry near Telham Hill at nine o'clock. The Normans advanced to the attack immediately, before the small English army was even drawn up in battle array. It was a hard-fought battle, in which the Normans had to throw in one mounted attack after another against the English front, but at the end of the day Harold was killed, and his remaining followers fled from the field.

Nearly forty at the time of the invasion, William the Conqueror had overcome the handicap of his illegitimate birth to make good his claim to the dukedom, and had forcefully and skillfully restored order to the strife-ridden duchy. Remembered as a ruthlessly ambitious warlord, William was also a pious Christian, and his campaign against Harold Godwinson was in the nature of a crusade. Two years earlier, in 1064, Harold had crossed the Channel, been captured by an enemy, and then rescued by William. For reasons not altogether clear, perhaps out of gratitude, Harold thereupon took an oath to uphold William's claim to the English crown. Back in England at the death of

Edward, Harold chose to ignore that oath when he had himself crowned at Westminster Abbey. William's subsequent expedition to the island kingdom — to punish the "oath-breaker" — had the backing of the pope.

The Norman victory at Hastings, however, did not end William's crusade; he could not yet consider himself master of the kingdom. The English leaders refused to submit: the earls of Northumbria and Mercia withdrew to the north with the idea of proclaiming King Edward's young nephew, Edgar, as Harold's successor; both the Archbishop of Canterbury and the Archbishop of York supported the proclamation of Edgar; King Edward's widow remained in control of the old West Saxon capital of Winchester; and the gates of London, already by far the most important town in the entire country, were closed against him.

Indeed, William recognized, as the Romans and the Saxon King Alfred had recognized before him, that London was the key to the island, and that no man could control England until London was in his power. For London was the very heart of the country's system of communications. The roads from the north, from the Midlands, and from East Anglia all converged there, to cross the Thames over London Bridge. These roads then linked up with the roads that led east to Canterbury, west to Winchester, and south to the Channel ports.

Canterbury submitted to William toward the end of October and Queen Edith handed over Winchester in November. But until London fell, the Duke of Normandy could never become King of England.

William realized that London was far too strong to be taken by direct attack with the few thousand knights and archers he had at his disposal — even had he dared to risk antagonizing the city's rich merchants and influential citizens by attempting to do so. Its defenses were formidable; its army, trained and tested in the fight against the Vikings during previous centuries, was the best equipped in the country.

Rather than assault the city, William decided therefore to surround it. First he moved up to Southwark, the suburb that had developed on the bank of the Thames at the southern end of London Bridge. Then, having thrown back a force of Edgar's supporters that galloped out of the city to oppose him, he set fire to the wooden buildings of Southwark before moving along the south bank of the river into Berkshire. Devastating the country as he passed, he rode on to Wallingford, where he crossed to the far bank of the Thames, and then moved northeast to Berkhampstead.

By thus isolating their capital, William had demonstrated to the English leaders the pointlessness of further resistance. First the Archbishop of Canterbury submitted to him, then the Archbishop of York, then Edgar and the earls of Northumbria and Mercia, and finally, in the words of a chronicler, "all the chief men of London, and they gave hostages to him, and he promised that he would be a gracious liege lord."

William entered the capital shortly before Christmas. On Christmas Day he was crowned King of England in Westminster Abbey.

He had conquered England, but his more demanding task now was to hold it. His cavalry, expert in fighting pitched battles and in rounding up and destroying local levies in the open countryside, was of little use in operations against walled towns. By themselves the

ET VENIT AD PEVENESÆ:

N PRELIO:

cavalrymen could do little to subdue and control whole districts of disaffected and unruly people. William had learned on the Continent that to hold down an area successfully, it was essential to build a castle in a commanding position, not only to overawe the inhabitants of the surrounding countryside, but also to serve as a garrison and supply base, and as a fortified center of administration. Castles had accordingly been built all over northern France from Dol to Abbeville, from Fécamp to Sées, and custody of them had been entrusted only to those whose loyalty to the ducal house was unquestioned.

Some of the bigger castles were of stone, but many were of wood. These timber fortresses were quite simple in design. Built on an earthen mound, surrounded by a ditch, they comprised a tall tower enclosed on all sides by a palisaded rampart. The ditch was usually filled with water, and a drawbridge led across it to the castle's single gate. In the days following William's coronation, castles like this began to appear all over England: at Pevensey and Hastings in the south; at Exeter in the west; at Cambridge, Huntingdon, and Lincoln in the east; at Warwick, Nottingham, and Rockingham in the Midlands; at York in the north.

London was soon surrounded by a whole ring of castles, and in London itself orders were given by William for the construction, to begin immediately, of "three strongholds against the fickleness of the vast and fierce populace." Two of the strongholds William ordered were built in the southwest corner of the town: Montfichet's Tower, somewhere on the rising ground to the right bank of the Fleet River, which discharged its waters into the Thames three-

quarters of a mile downstream from London Bridge; and Baynard's Castle, a little farther downstream on the Thames waterfront itself. These two castles were relatively unimportant. The principal stronghold of the city was to be above London Bridge; and there was little doubt as to where that fortress should be sited.

In the days when Londinium was the capital of Britannia, an outlying province of the Roman Empire, the city had been enclosed by three miles of strong stone walls, about eight feet thick at their base and up to twenty feet in height. And at the southeastern angle of these walls, where the ground rose above the level of the wooden trestle bridge across the Thames, there were three bastions overlooking the river. Indeed, some men said that Julius Caesar himself had chosen the site of the most easterly of these three bastions for a fortress to command the bridge and the city. This fortress had been destroyed when Boudicca, Queen of the Iceni tribesmen from Norfolk, had fallen upon the town and burned it to the ground in A.D. 61 in revenge for her family's treatment at the hands of Roman soldiers. Certainly the little hill on the northern bank of the river at this place seemed to the Norman leaders an obvious site for their important new castle.

Work on the castle began soon after William's coronation, and within three months, the wooden structure of tower and palisaded rampart in the characteristic Norman manner seems to have been finished. At any rate, William considered London sufficiently well secured to leave England in March 1067, and to return home to Normandy where his gifted wife Matilda had

Three months after his coronation William I left England for the Continent, and in the years that followed he divided his time and his energies more or less equally between his native Normandy and his newly conquered island kingdom. In this thirteenth-century manuscript illumination, William is shown deeding Continental fiefs to his nephew the Count of Brittany.

been left in control of the duchy. He took with him Edward's nephew, Edgar, the earls of Northumbria and Mercia, and Stigand, Archbishop of Canterbury, so that there should remain behind, during his absence, no English leader powerful enough to dispute the control of his Norman deputies and garrison. And he sailed from Pevensey in a ship fitted with white sails in honor of the great victory that he had won and the peace that he had secured.

On his return to England later that year, William instituted the building of more castles. Year by year the number of these castles grew until by the end of the century at least eighty-four had been built in all parts of the country, most of them still of wood. Determined that the capital should have a castle as fine and formidable as any in the land, the king gave orders for his original wooden structure to be pulled down and for a larger, stronger tower to be built in its place.

The architect he chose for this task — according to some authorities — was Gundulf, a pious, emotional, yet business-like monk, whose great talents as a designer of both churches and fortresses were widely renowned. Gundulf had been born near Roüen about 1024, and he began his long and successful career as a clerk of the cathedral there. He vowed to become a monk during a storm at sea when he was on his way back to France after a pilgrimage to Jerusalem, and he soon proved himself as devout a monk as he had been conscientious as a clerk, frequently bursting into tears in the fervor of his religious feeling. In the Abbey at Bec Gundulf became a devoted friend of Lanfranc, who was then prior and who brought Gundulf to England with him on his appointment as Stigand's successor as

Archbishop of Canterbury. And it was probably while he was serving at Canterbury, as the highly efficient steward of the cathedral's estates, that Gundulf was employed to design the Tower of London.

While supervising the building operations in London, Gundulf is said to have lodged with a rich citizen named Eadmer Anhoende, who was immediately drawn, as Lanfranc had been, to the monk's pleasant and generous nature. In 1077 Gundulf was consecrated Bishop of Rochester. He remained at Rochester for over thirty years until his death at the age of eighty-four. He was buried in the beautiful cathedral there, which he had so carefully and lovingly rebuilt.

The Tower of London, presumably designed by Gundulf, was not a beautiful building — nor was it meant to be. It was intended to be awe-inspiring and formidable, to dominate the city and impress its citizens with the power of their Norman conquerors. Immensely thick walls, constructed of vast slabs of pale-colored limestone imported from the quarries of Caen and of hard, coarse ragstone brought upriver from Kent, towered to an enormous height. Pierced by the thin slits which were all that the exigencies of military architecture could allow for windows, the walls were topped by four turrets, three rectangular and one rounded. It was a nearly square building, 118 feet by 107 feet (with an apsidal projection at the southeast corner for the chapel), the flatness of its outer walls broken only by the buttresses that rose from ground to battlements. Some time after its completion, the Tower was whitewashed so that it appeared more enormous than ever, the unmistakable master of the city upon whose buildings, mostly of wood, it so forbiddingly

looked down. The whitewash has gone now and the Norman slits have been replaced by wide glazed windows, but the essential structure of the White Tower, as it is still known, remains unchanged after almost nine centuries.

Originally the main entrance was on the western front, on an upper floor facing the city, with an outer wall concealing both the gateway itself and the steps leading up to it. Internally each floor was divided into major apartments: above the entrance floor were the banqueting hall, the sword room, and the chapel; and above these again were the council chamber and the gallery of the chapel. From every apartment the garrison, whose barracks were on the lower floor, could keep watch on the river and bridge, the city and the surrounding countryside. And in times of trouble, the soldiers could shoot their arrows and hurl their missiles down upon the king's rebellious subjects through the high loopholes.

The first stage of the building was completed in 1078; but after 1091, when the Tower was "by tempest and wind sore shaken," the Conqueror's son, William Rufus, repaired and strengthened it. Rufus's brother and successor, Henry I, carried out further repairs and improvements; and, during the reigns of his successors, in particular those of Henry III (1216–72) and Edward I (1272–1307), there was built around the Norman fortress a series of bastions, gateways, towers, and protective walls that made the Tower of London one of the largest and most invulnerable strongholds in Europe. Indeed, it was considered one of the principal wonders of Europe, a marvel of military architecture soaring above the roofs of England's capital.

As late as the mid-sixteenth century, when this ink sketch of the London skyline was executed by a Dutch artist, the semicircular contour of the capital's original Roman walls was still visible. Gazing north from the teeming Thames-side suburb of Southwark, the artist could see not only the Tower and its outbuildings but the numerous churches and palaces of the city of London as well.

Medieval London was still almost entirely enclosed within its ancient Roman walls. Outside each gate there were clusters of ragged buildings, small monasteries and hostelries, groups of huntsmen's kennels, and fencing schools. The suburb of Southwark — the wild disorderly haunt of drunkards, rakes, and whores — was growing along the southern bank of the river where fishermen's and boatmen's hovels, brothels, and taverns were huddled along the waterfront. There was also a gradually extending line of rich men's mansions and bishops' palaces along the country road that led from the southwest gate of the city, Ludgate, to the royal palace and abbey of Westminster. But the great majority of London's inhabitants — about 30,000 or 40,000 toward the end of the twelfth century — lived within the semicircular area of 326 acres enclosed by the high Roman walls.

They lived together in perfect harmony, wrote William FitzStephen, secretary and biographer of Thomas à Becket (1118–70), in the earliest detailed account of the city that has survived. FitzStephen, like his hero Becket, was born in twelfth-century London and to him the city was a place of perfect delight and constant enchantment. He praised the excellence of the fish that teemed in the sparkling waters of the river and the succulence of the tender meats so cunningly roasted in the public cook shops and covered with the hotly spiced sauces that were so pleasing to the medieval palate. He delighted in the gardens and orchards of the monasteries, and the pastures and meadows beyond the walls where, beside the numerous fresh streams, the mill wheels turned with "merry din." He extolled the industry of the healthy, good-looking citizens — the craftsmen at their benches, the young students in the schools, the priests at their devotions, the apprentices practicing archery and tilting at a target on a post, the virtuous ladies at their spinning wheels.

Most of the people lived in houses of wood. Indeed, despite an enactment in 1189 requiring the lower part of all houses to be built of stone and their roofs to be tiled, the subsequent (constantly repeated) official condemnations of timber walls and roofs of reed, stubble, rushes, and straw indicate that London remained predominantly a town of wood and plaster throughout the Middle Ages. Yet by the time of Henry III's accession in 1216 there were several stone buildings in London that were as fine as any to be found in northern Europe. Most admired among them were the magnificent stone bridge across the Thames, begun in 1176 and finished in 1209, and St. Paul's Cathedral, a beautiful building replacing the wooden church destroyed in a fire that ravaged London in 1135. And rising above them all was the massive, forbidding Tower, whose walls — since pulverized Roman red tiles and bricks had been used in their construction — looked to the awe-inspired beholder as though they had been "built with mortars tempered with the blood of beasts."

During the reign of Henry III, the area enclosed by the outer walls of the fortress buildings extended to more than twelve acres. Outside the walls was a wide, deep moat; and on the southern side, between the moat and the river, was a long wharf, piled high with bales and cases, barrels and jars. Inside the walls there was by then a fine palace as well as a towering fortress;

for at least as early as 1140, when King Stephen's court celebrated Whitsuntide there, the Tower of London had become known as one of the principal residences of the English monarchs. It was also — as well as being a fortress and a garrison — an armory, a jewel house, a wardrobe, a mint, a menagerie, and a state prison.

A thirteenth-century visitor approaching Henry III's Tower from the city to the west would first come to an outwork, or barbican, known as the Lion Tower, since it was there that the king's wild animals were kept (see map, pages 26–27). He would ride across the stone causeway and the wooden drawbridge that spanned the outer moat, then cross another drawbridge to pass beneath the raised portcullis of the Middle Tower. Beyond the Middle Tower a causeway and a third drawbridge stretched 125 feet across the inner moat to the Byward Tower, the gate house to the outer ward, which — like the Middle Tower — was protected by an iron portcullis. Beyond the Byward Tower, guarding the approaches to the inner ward, was the Bell Tower, so-called because it housed the warning bell that called the garrison to arms.

Turning north past the Bell Tower, beneath the high curtain walls of the outer ward, the medieval visitor would pass on his right the first of the twelve towers built into the inner curtain wall, all except one of which can still be seen today, though altered in varying degrees over the ensuing centuries. This first tower was completely rebuilt by Henry III's son, Edward I, at the very end of the thirteenth century. It takes its present name, the Beauchamp Tower, from Thomas Beauchamp, third Earl of Warwick, who was imprisoned there in 1397.

Riding on around the outer ward the horseman would next come upon Robyn the Devylls Tower (later to be known as Devereux Tower after its most famous prisoner, Robert Devereux, second Earl of Essex), then four other towers in the northern wall: Flint Tower (which contained the most dank and noisome dungeons in the entire fortress and was alternatively known as Little Hell), Bowyer Tower (where the king's bowmaker had his workrooms and lodgings), Brick Tower, and Martin Tower (where the crown jewels and royal regalia were kept). Now turning south, the rider would come to Constable Tower, Broad Arrow Tower, and at the southeastern angle of the wall, Salt Tower, formerly known as Julius Caesar's Tower since it was supposed that the Romans had built their first wooden fortress on this site.

Next to Salt Tower was Lanthorn Tower, and next to that, at the western end of the royal apartments, Hall Tower, the ground floor of which served as a guardroom to the entrance to the Great Hall. After 1360 when the records of the kingdom were transferred there from the White Tower, Hall Tower was also known as Record Tower. It is now more usually called Wakefield Tower after William de Wakefield, King's Clerk to Edward III.

Opposite Hall Tower was St. Thomas's Tower, which contained a small chapel dedicated to Thomas à Becket. This, a tower of uncompromising starkness, stood guard over the gloomy Traitor's Gate, the main entrance into the fortress from the river and the one used by prisoners returning to their dungeons after their trials in Westminster Hall.

Passing St. Thomas's Tower on his left, the rider

would then come to Garden Tower, a square squat building overlooking the constable's garden. To be known to later generations as the Bloody Tower — for it was there that the boy-king Edward V and his brother were to be murdered — Garden Tower was built by Henry III as a handsome gateway into the inner ward. So, turning right beneath its vaulted roof and raised portcullis, the horseman would come at last upon the massive walls of the White Tower immediately in front of him. To his right were the gardens and buildings of the royal apartments stretching along the line of the Roman wall as far as the Wardrobe Tower, which faced the east window of the Chapel of St. John; to his left were other gardens and beyond them the small Chapel of St. Peter.

The attractive, colorful appearance of the inner ward was in pleasant contrast to the foreboding outer walls and bastions of the fortress. There the busy life of a medieval palace was seen in all its variety. One must imagine not just the stone buildings that can still be seen today, but a conglomeration of wooden structures, tents and awnings, penthouses, stables, and covered ways, most of them gaily painted and all of them surrounded by the numerous servants and attendants of the court, and by the piemakers, fishmongers, and other tradesmen from the nearby city who thronged the inner ward in the hope of obtaining an order for their wares. There would have been a large kitchen, outside which cattle, poultry, and pigs were kept in a courtyard awaiting the attention of the butcher and the cook. There would also have been a dairy and a pigeon loft, a brewery, a bakery and a forge, beehives, fruit stores, and sheds for the gardeners.

Thirteenth- and fourteenth-century additions to the Tower of London made the fortress one of Europe's most formidable citadels by 1597, as this engraving clearly indicates. A key at right identifies the numerous towers, gardens, and gates. Many — such as the Tower at the Gate (B), now known as Byward Tower — have been renamed over the course of subsequent centuries.

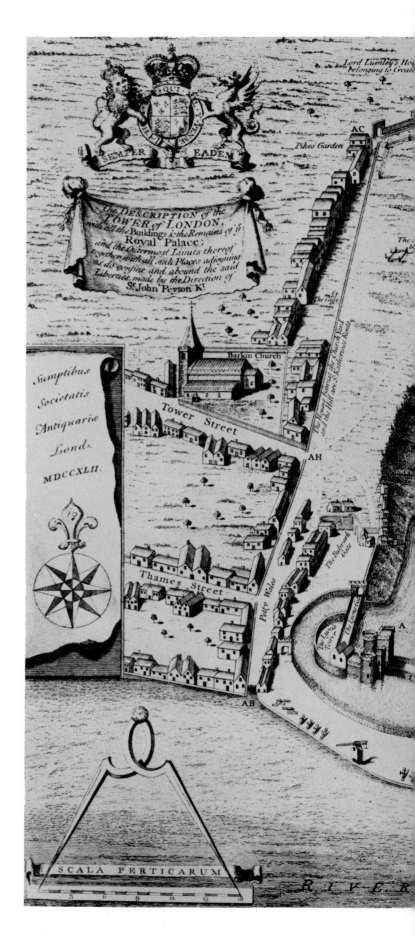

The gardens in any palace were of the greatest importance, not only for the growing of flowers and vegetables but also for the cultivation of herbs, essential ingredients in medieval cookery. Mustard and parsley, cumin for flavoring poultry, fennel for flavoring fish, coriander for preserves, and anise for meat jellies would all certainly have been planted in the gardens of the Tower. Other herbs, spices, and aromatic roots that could not easily be grown in England would have been imported. Cinnamon from the East, saffron from Spain, ginger, galingale, zedoary, pepper, nutmeg, and mace were all imported in large quantities in the thirteenth century and were used with a liberality that would outrage the modern palate. Being expensive they would have been kept, together with the palace's supplies of sugar, rice, almonds, and Spanish and Italian dried fruits, in the Wardrobe Tower. For the Wardrobe was not only used as a store for valuable clothes and as the tailors' workroom, but for the safekeeping of plate and jewels and such precious condiments and exotic foods as might tempt the pilferer.

Although the pestle and the mortar required much time and effort, they were among the most vital utensils in the medieval kitchen. However, not all the meals prepared by the cooks received the same careful and expensive treatment. Indeed, this would have been impossible, for when the peripatetic court came for one of its seasonal visits to the Tower, the number of its retinue was prodigious. The numbers had to be prodigious, since the royal household, after all, was the government of the country.

The most important household officials — the Lord High Steward, the Lord High Chancellor, the Lord

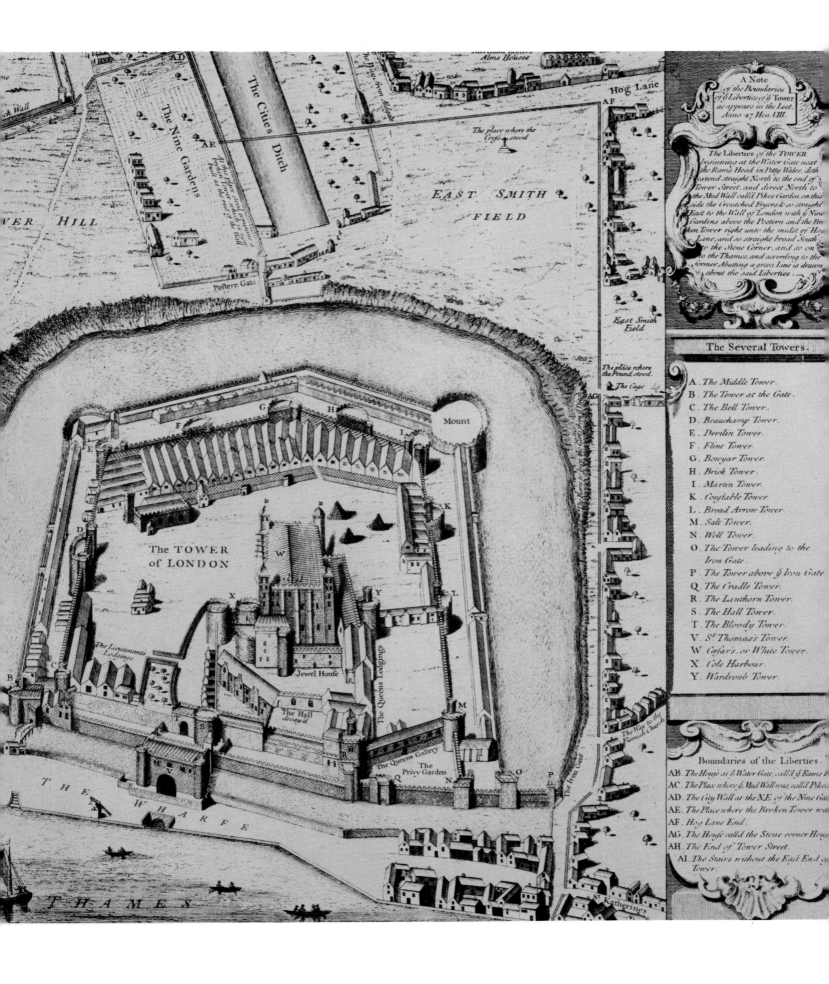

High Treasurer, the Lord Great Chamberlain, the Lord High Constable, the Keeper of the Seals, and the King's Marshal — were also the most powerful officers of state. All of them had a duty to attend the king and all of them had their own large train of servants and attendants. Also, in their several departments were a host of lesser officials — the Chamberlain of the Candles, the Keeper of the Tents, the Master Steward of the Larder, the Usher of the Spithouse, the Marshal of the Trumpets, the Keeper of the Books, the Keeper of the Dishes and of the Cups, the Steward of the Buttery, the cat hunters, the wolf catchers — as well as clerks and limners, carters, water carriers, washerwomen and laundresses, chaplains, lawyers, archers, huntsmen, hornblowers, barbers, minstrels, guards and servitors, bakers and confectioners. And all had to be fed.

As far as the king's family, immediate circle, and most distinguished guests were concerned, the main meal of the day, dinner, was served at about eleven o'clock in the morning in the Great Hall, which was on the south side of the inner ward to the east of the Garden Tower. The members of the court and their guests would first wash their hands, holding them out to the servants who poured hot water over them from bronze or pottery ewers, catching the water in bowls. Having dried their hands, the guests would take their places at table. Silver plate, silver spoons, and cups of horn, crystal, maple wood, or silver were laid upon the white cloth, but each guest provided himself with his own knife, which was kept in a leather sheath attached to a belt or girdle. The food was brought to the table in numerous dishes by a procession of servitors, every dish containing enough for two people: the gentlemen helped the ladies, and the young, their seniors — placing the food in trenchers, scooped-out half loaves of bread that were afterwards distributed to the poor. The king had a particularly generous helping of food, so that he could offer tasty looking morsels to favored guests.

There would commonly be as many as six meat courses, with as many as four or five different dishes in each course, followed by a course of sweetmeats, confectionary, and fruit. On Fridays, of course, the dishes would be fish, and there would be fewer of them. Wine, most of it imported, accompanied every course; beer and cider were normally drunk only by the inferior denizens of the court and water was considered unwholesome. The wine cup was handed around the table from guest to guest and was frequently replenished from the numerous ewers on the board.

Dinner, an important social occasion as well as a great feast, was a prolonged meal and a formal one. But breakfast, except for children, comprised no more than a piece of bread and a cup of wine, taken after the daily morning mass in one of the fortress's chapels. And supper was a light meal with but a few insubstantial courses — although, as at dinner, a plenitude of wine.

The Great Hall, in which dinner and supper were served and in which at other times the ladies and gentlemen of the court met to talk and entertain themselves, was a gaily — a modern eye might think gaudily — colored room. Contemporary taste demanded the most resplendent colors in domestic, as well as in ecclesiastical, interiors.

There is no evidence to show what the Great Hall at the Tower of London looked like, either inside or outside, but it was certainly immense, covering the whole

Q uant plus su longh de li amors plu
T ous su sien sans pchon diex wint
E nsi me va damors ensi mon tens

of the main upper floor of the royal apartments. There was, no doubt, a dais at one end where the royal family sat, at least one and probably two or more large fireplaces, and tall screens around the doors and other apertures to keep out the drafts. The records show that Henry III spent a great deal of the royal revenue on paint, and that many interiors decorated for him were generously garnished with gold stars, green and red lions, and painted flowers, particularly the rose of Provence in honor of his queen, Eleanor, daughter of Raymond Berenger IV, Count of Provence.

Furnishings in the Great Hall, as in other apartments, were presumably sparse. The hall may well have had little in it other than the great tables and benches, chairs, serving boards, painted cloth hangings, and perhaps carpets. The royal bedchambers above the hall might have contained a few chairs and iron-bound chests, a trestle table or two, a tall candlestick, a row of pegs on the wall — used as a perch by the royal falcons as well as for hanging clothes — and, of course, in each of them, a great bed, the most valued piece of furniture in every palace as in every house. The king's bed would have been a huge piece with a feather mattress and a fur coverlet, surrounded by linen hangings that could be pulled back during the day. His grooms slept on trundle beds in the same room, other officials of the household outside the door. The queen likewise shared her bedchamber with several of her ladies, who also slept on trundle beds.

The bedchamber was used for bathing as well as for sleeping. Round, deep tubs were brought into the room by servants who poured the hot water into the tub while the bather was already sitting down inside. Baths were not taken regularly but Henry III was renowned for his strong views on cleanliness and sanitation and tubs were more often in use in his time than in the days of his predecessors. There are known to have been privies, adjoining the bedchambers and emptying through drainage shafts into the moat, in other thirteenth-century castles; although no record of them survives, there were almost certainly such privies at the Tower also.

In the winter the court usually retired early after games of chess or dice or listening to the songs of minstrels around the fire. Sometimes the gentlemen would leave the ladies embroidering while they enjoyed a late supper, more often than not an excuse to get drunk. Occasionally there was dancing or a display by jugglers and acrobats, or an evening of storytelling by a minstrel who knew by heart the ever popular romances and legends of King Arthur, Guinevere, and Lancelot. In the summer there were games of bowls to enjoy on the Tower lawns, and tournaments. Above all there was hunting, both with hounds and with hawks, which was the delight of ladies and gentlemen alike, and of young and old.

The huntsmen, clattering across the causeways and drawbridges and out through the Lion Tower, would soon be in the country. For it was not until the middle of the sixteenth century that London began to spread beyond the ancient Roman walls to any great extent. Game abounded in Moorfields, in Tothill Fields and Smithfield; and in the woods beyond the little villages of Hampstead and Islington, the courtiers and officers of the Tower rode with their falcons and hounds and chased the wild deer through the clearings.

II

TIMES OF TROUBLE

Henry III had made the Tower as attractive and comfortable as any palace in England, but his taste for colorful decoration and luxurious living had never been allowed to interfere with the need to ensure that it also remained the strongest of fortresses. For despite the gaiety of the court in times of peace and quiet, there were many other times when Henry was forced to shut himself up behind the Tower's walls to protect himself from his rebellious people.

Nowhere in William FitzStephen's delightful account of the twelfth-century city he so much loved is there more than a hint of the violence and turbulence of medieval London, or of the part that the constable and the garrison of the Tower had constantly to play in keeping the unruly citizens in order in the name of the king. Yet only a few years earlier, in the troubled reign of William the Conqueror's grandson, King Stephen, the Londoners had risen in revolt and had swarmed around the Tower in their thousands, threatening to seize it and to kill the royal officers. And only a few years after FitzStephen's death the citizens had again been at the gates, this time under the leadership of the barons, protesting against the tyranny of William's great-great-grandson, King John. And then, in the reign of John's son, Henry III, the Tower came under violent attack by partisans of Simon de Montfort, the Earl of Leicester, who was determined to curb the king's power.

Henry was repeatedly obliged to seek refuge in the Tower when Montfort and his supporters, encouraged by the citizens of London, threatened the king's power in the capital. Once, when Montfort's partisans were encamped outside London at Richmond — while the king's son, Prince Edward, was far away fighting the Welsh — Henry had to lock himself up in the Tower with his wife, Queen Eleanor. And he was forced to remain there by crowds of armed citizens thronging around the gates.

Prince Edward hurried back from Wales to Windsor Castle, and Eleanor determined to join her son there. The queen slipped out of the fortress by one of the river gates, stepped into her barge, and was rowed vigorously upstream by her oarsmen. But she had scarcely covered half a mile when a rabble collected on London Bridge, pelted her with stones and rotten eggs and mud, and forced her to seek safety within the precincts of St. Paul's.

Two years later Simon de Montfort's collaborators took possession of the Tower and managed to retain it until 1265, when Prince Edward defeated Montfort at Evesham and thereby enabled the king to return. However, Henry's severe treatment of the leaders of the defeated army, his confiscation of their estates, and the welcome he extended to the papal legate, Cardinal Ottobuono, led them once more into revolt under the leadership of the Earl of Gloucester. Ottobuono, who had been sent to England by the pope to punish various English bishops for supporting Montfort against the king, had taken up residence in the Tower. There he was besieged by Gloucester, whose army had occupied London. But the Tower garrison contrived to hold out until King Henry arrived to relieve them. After rescuing Ottobuono, Henry reinforced the garrison and appointed a new constable.

By then the office of Constable of the Tower was one of the most honorable and desirable in the king's gift. It was also one of the most profitable. Numerous perquisites were attached to it: every boat that came upstream toward the city had to moor at Tower Wharf to unload "such a quantitie of rushes as a persone could holde betwene his armes"; every boat carrying oysters, cockles, or mussels had to deposit one maund [a varying unit of weight up to 82.286 pounds] upon the wharf; every boat carrying wine from Bordeaux or elsewhere had to leave two flagons for the constable's cellar. All swans swimming out to sea under London Bridge belonged to the constable, as did all the horses, oxen, cows, pigs, and sheep that either fell off the bridge or swam across the river toward the Tower. For every foot of these animals that stumbled into the moat the constable received a penny; and every cart, empty or laden, that fell in became his property. The herbage growing on Tower Hill all belonged to him.

He was entitled to demand six shillings, eight pence a year from the owners of all boats fishing for sprat between the Tower and the sea; one shilling a year from all ships carrying herring to London from Yarmouth or from abroad; two pence from each pilgrim who came to London by sea to worship at the shrine of Saint James. He was also entitled to demand fees for the "suite of his irons" from the Tower's prisoners, from twenty pounds a year for a duke to five pounds a year for a knight. All prisoners of the rank of knight and above were, in addition, required to pay generously for their food and accommodation.

During the last years of the reign of Henry III and throughout the reign of Edward I, who continued his father's work in improving its fortifications, the Tower remained in royal hands. But in the time of King Edward's son, Edward II, it was seized by Lord Mortimer — the violent lover of Queen Isabella (wife of Edward II) — who beheaded the constable, released the prisoners, and gave the keys to the citizens of London. After Edward II was murdered at Berkeley Castle in 1327, the country was governed by Mortimer and Queen Isabella, while Edward III, fourteen years old at the time of his accession, was kept a virtual prisoner in the Tower. Before he was eighteen, however, the new king had displayed those remarkable talents that were to bring him such striking victories over the Scots and the French. He had Mortimer arrested and executed and had his mother banished to Castle Rising in Norfolk.

When Edward III died in 1377, his gifted son the Black Prince was already dead; and so another boy-king came to the throne, and once more the security of the Tower was threatened. The new king, Richard II, son of the Black Prince, seemed as "beautiful as an arch-angel" when, at the age of ten, he came forth from the Tower clothed all in white and proceeded to West-minster Abbey for his coronation through streets decorated with tapestries and banners and lined with cheering crowds. But within three years the incompetent government of Richard's council, led by his uncle John of Gaunt, Duke of Lancaster, had so enraged the people that in 1381 over 100,000 men from Essex and Kent marched upon London.

The grievances of the marchers were many, and they were determined to have them redressed. Their revolt had been precipitated by the poll tax, a method of extracting money from the poor for the war against France, but their discontent went deeper than that. It had its roots in social rather than political causes: the

rebels demanded an end to the servitude of the peasants, freedom from the obligation of giving their personal services to the landlords — as they were required to do as villeins — and the right to hold land by paying a money rent for it instead. In sympathy with their demands, or at least sharing their dislike of the government, the apprentices of London and various democratically minded aldermen welcomed the rebels at the approaches to the city and opened the gates for them. The king's ministers, the officials of the royal household, and all those who had cause to fear the anger of the mob fled for safety to the Tower.

King Richard's mother, Queen Joan, "the fair maid of Kent," was at the Tower, along with his uncle the Earl of Buckingham, youngest son of Edward III, and the king's cousin, Henry. The earls of Suffolk, Kent, Salisbury, and Warwick were all there too, together with the Lord Treasurer, Sir Robert Hales; John Legge, who had devised the poll tax; the chancellor, Simon of Sudbury, who was also Archbishop of Canterbury; and Sir William Walworth, a fishmonger who was Mayor of London. John of Gaunt, Duke of Lancaster, was away from London at the time, attempting to negotiate a treaty with the Scots; but his palace, the Savoy — formerly the London palace of the Count of Savoy, uncle of Henry III's queen, Eleanor of Provence — was attacked by the mob who killed the guards and set the building on fire.

The mob also attacked and destroyed the Fleet and Marshalsea prisons, liberating all those who were confined in them. Its members attacked the Archbishop of Canterbury's palace at Lambeth, burning some of the buildings and throwing the chancery records that were stored there into the flames. They rampaged into New Temple to burn the lawyers' rolls and to demolish more houses, including the mansion of the Lord Treasurer, Hales. They stormed into kitchens for food and into cellars for wine. They set fire to numerous houses belonging to lawyers, courtiers, and the clergy. They broke into the mansions of the city merchants and tumbled their contents out into the streets.

"Rushing into the houses that were the best provisioned," recorded the chronicler Jean Froissart, "they fell on the food and drink that they found. In the hope of appeasing them, nothing was refused them. . . . They destroyed several fine houses and threatened those who had closed the gates of London Bridge, saying that they would burn all the suburbs, take London by force, and burn and destroy everything."

The leader of the mob, Wat Tyler, a man of obscure origin who seems to have come from Kent and may once have been a soldier, marched at its head upon the house of a rich citizen named Richard Lyon against whom Tyler had conceived a grudge. The rioters broke into the house, murdered Lyon, cut off his head, and paraded it through the burning streets on a pike. That night they encamped in St. Catherine's Square before the Tower, announcing that they would not leave London until they had got all they wanted, and threatening the life of Archbishop Sudbury, the chancellor, if he did not give them a satisfactory account of all the revenue levied in England for the last five years.

From a high window in one of the turrets of the White Tower, the fourteen-year-old king looked down upon the mob, "howling like men possessed," and upon the flames and smoke that leaped into the sky above

The cartoon quality of these fifteenth-century Flemish miniatures belies the deep seriousness of the event they depict — Wat Tyler's 1381 rebellion. In the view opposite, the boy-king Richard II valiantly confronts the massed peasants. The same panel also shows Richard's futile attempt (left center) to prevent Tyler's assassination. In the king's absence, a group of rebels (above) storms the White Tower and captures several of Richard's ministers, who were later beheaded.

the city. He was advised by the mayor, Sir William Walworth, to give orders to the Tower garrison, and to all those Londoners who remained loyal to the crown, to arm themselves with the sharpest and heaviest weapons that they could find and to fall upon the rebels as they lay in a drunken sleep in the streets. Only one in twenty of the rebels would be armed, the mayor believed, and it would be possible to kill them off like flies. There were six hundred men at arms and six hundred archers in the Tower; these alone, Walworth said, could slaughter the rioters with impunity.

At a council held that night, however, some of the king's other advisers, in particular the aged Earl of Salisbury, disagreed. "Sir, if you appease the mob with fair words, that would be better," Salisbury said. "Grant them all they ask, for if we begin something we cannot finish, nothing will ever be recovered, for us or for our heirs, and England will be a desert."

The next morning, June 14, the Friday following the feast of Corpus Christi, the king appeared on the roof of one of the bastions overlooking Tower Hill and called out to the rebels that if they returned peaceably to their homes all of them would be pardoned. As a token of his good faith, Richard sealed a charter of pardon in their sight and had it sent down to them by two of his knights, who read it aloud at the gates. Yet most of the rebels, shouting their refusal of the pardon, turned away from the Tower and went back into the city to continue with their work of destruction.

Others, however, accepted the king's brave offer to meet them in a meadow at Mile End, where their grievances could be discussed. And thus, accompanied by only a few attendants and the mayor, Richard rode

out from the Tower toward the meeting place. Before he left, he advised Archbishop Sudbury and other ministers whose lives had been threatened to seize the opportunity, escape from the Tower by one of the water gates, and slip away downstream. But as Sudbury appeared on the river stairs he was recognized by the rebels, still congregating in the thousands on Catherine's Hill, and he was forced to retreat inside the walls.

The peasant rebels, and the London ruffians who had joined them in search of plunder and the pleasures of violence, did not leave Sudbury there in peace. Storming across the causeway and drawbridges, they pushed their way through the gates which, for some reason that has never been satisfactorily explained, were left undefended by the 1,200-man garrison. They poured into the outer ward, across the curtain walls, and through the gateway of the Garden Tower into the inner bailey. They pushed their way into the Great Hall and into the Wardrobe, ransacking the kitchens, the bedchambers, and the armory. They forced down the door of the queen mother's private apartments and smashed her furniture, tore down the hangings from the walls, and cut her bedclothes into ribbons. The queen herself escaped. Smuggled out of the Tower in the confusion by her pages, she was rowed away upstream, to the security of the Norman riverside stronghold, Baynard's Castle.

The king's ministers, however, did not escape. While the soldiers of the garrison stood back against the walls — believing, so it was afterwards given as an excuse, that the king had agreed to allow the mob to bring its enemies to justice — the shouting rabble streamed into the White Tower and climbed the steps to the Chapel

of St. John, where they found Archbishop Sudbury, Treasurer Hales, John Legge, and John of Gaunt's physician at prayer. All four of them were dragged from the altar, down the steps, and out of the gates onto Tower Hill. There they were beheaded, and their heads stuck on pikes and carried in triumph through the streets of the city.

At Mile End, meanwhile, the king was making promises to the rebels who had gathered there: they would be pardoned, he told them, and emancipated from villeinage; they would be permitted to rent land at fourpence an acre. Trusting in the young king's word — which he, perhaps, and his council, certainly, were determined should not be kept — many of the rebels went home.

Wat Tyler and his Kentish followers, however, remained in London, and Richard agreed to see them the next day at Smithfield, the open land northwest of the Tower where horse sales were held in more peaceful times. At Smithfield, promises similar to those made at Mile End were given to the men of Kent. But Tyler declared himself unsatisfied. His days as leader of so powerful a mob had led him to believe that he could achieve far more. He spurred on his horse and rode right up to the king "so that his horse's tail was under the very nose of the King's horse."

"King," he said to him insolently, "do you see all these men here?"

"Yes. Why do you ask?" replied Richard.

"They are all under my orders, and have all sworn to obey my commands."

Tyler then listed his further demands: the end of all lordship except that of the king, the confiscation of the estates of the church, the abolition of bishoprics. To all these demands, the king readily assented and then asked Tyler to take his men home. But Tyler was suspicious. He distrusted the readiness of the assent to his requests and noticed the restiveness of the king's retinue. Riding up to the guard who was holding Richard's sword in his hand, he said, "Give me that sword."

"I will not," replied the guard. "It is the King's sword, and you are not fit to hold it. You are only a laborer. If you and I were alone here," he added, pointing to St. Paul's, "you would not have spoken like that for a pile of gold as big as that church."

"I swear," shouted Tyler, "I will not eat another meal until I have your head."

At this, the mayor lost his temper. Riding forward and calling Tyler a "stinking wretch" to speak like that in the king's presence, he knocked him clean off his horse with the flat of his broadsword. As the rebel leader lay on the ground, one of the king's squires dismounted and stabbed him in the stomach, killing him. Seeing this, the peasants cried out in horror; brandishing their weapons, they advanced upon the king's retinue. With remarkable self-control Richard trotted forward to hold them back, calling out to them: "Sirs, will you kill your King? I am your captain, follow me." And so inbred was their reverence for the king, so accustomed had they grown under Tyler's leadership to obeying orders, that they did follow him, riding away after him to the north.

Walworth galloped back into the city to raise a volunteer force. Strengthening it with knights and archers from the Tower garrison, he rode back to the rebel force and surrounded it. The king spared the rebels' lives, but all the promises that had been made to them were ultimately broken, and the pardons granted by the king were ignored. The head of Wat Tyler took the place of Sudbury's on London Bridge.

Richard had displayed great courage during the Peasants' Revolt of 1381. He was later to display — as well as deep artistic sensibility and an almost effete fastidiousness — an aptitude for statesmanship. But the deaths of an adored wife and of most of his close friends seem to have unbalanced his judgment to such an extent that he was incapable of dealing with the problems and the enemies of his later years. At the age of thirty-two, in 1399, he was brought to the Tower as a prisoner, and in the Tower he was forced to sign his abdication.

"He entered the Great Hall in full kingly regalia, with the crown on his head and the sceptre in his hands," Froissart recorded. "He came in alone and unattended, and spoke as follows: 'I have been King of England, Duke of Aquitaine and Lord of Ireland for twenty-two years, and these thrones, dominions, and inheritances, together with this crown and sceptre, I now hand over freely to my cousin Henry of Lancaster.' "

So Henry, son of John of Gaunt, Duke of Lancaster, and grandson of Edward III, became King Henry IV, the first of the Lancastrian kings. (See chart, page 168.) Throughout his reign and that of his son, Henry V, the Tower remained secure in royal hands. In the reign of his grandson, Henry VI (1422–61), however, it once again came under attack by Kentish rebels.

This time the mob was led by Jack Cade, an Irishman by birth who had fled to France after murdering a pregnant woman and had joined the French army. On his return to England, Cade set himself up as a

physician in Kent under an assumed name and married the daughter of a squire. The rebellion that bears his name broke out in May 1450, when 40,000 men under his leadership marched upon London. Unlike the uprising of 1381, Cade's Rebellion was not directed against landowners, but against the oppressive officials of the king and, in particular, against the Lord Treasurer, Lord Saye-and-Sele, and his son-in-law, William Crowmer, Sheriff of Kent.

The rebels established themselves in Blackheath, south of the Thames, and immediately demanded the dismissal of these two men and several others from the king's service. At first this demand was refused, but after the king's army had been overwhelmed by the rebels, Henry VI retreated to Kenilworth, and the insurgents prepared to storm across London Bridge, to take the city and the Tower. On July 1 they entered Southwark, and Cade established his headquarters at the White Hart, entering the city the next day. There was no resistance to him, for many of the aldermen had as much reason to dislike the members of the royal household as he himself had.

From his new headquarters in the city, Cade demanded that Lord Saye-and-Sele should be brought out of the Tower and delivered up to him. This was done and his men promptly cut off the treasurer's head. William Crowmer was next arrested by the insurgents. He also was straightaway executed in Cade's presence. The two heads were fixed to poles, made to kiss each other, and carried through the streets. But the crisis of the rebellion was already past. Cade's excesses, the murder of other victims, and the robbery of several rich citizens turned the aldermen against him. Alarmed that the rebels would soon turn to the plunder of the entire city, the mayor appealed to the Constable of the Tower for protection.

The constable immediately assembled a large force at the southern end of London Bridge to prevent the re-entry into the city of Cade's men from their camp at Southwark. For a time it appeared as if the constable's force, strong as it was, would not be able to hold the rebels back. They stormed the bridge, pushed the defenders off the southern end into the river, and set fire to the drawbridge in the middle, proclaiming their intention of attacking the Tower. Reinforced by criminals whom they had released from the King's Bench and Marshalsea prisons, Cade's men attempted to rush the gate. They killed the constable and appeared to be at the point of victory on several occasions, but at nine o'clock on the morning of July 6, they were forced to give way. A few days later in the country, Cade was captured and mortally wounded by Crowmer's successor as Sheriff of Kent. The rebel leader died in a cart on his way back to London and four days later his head was cut off, his body cut into quarters, and the remains were dragged around London on a hurdle to remind the citizens of a traitor's fate.

The unfortunate king's troubles did not end with the death of Cade, for his later reign saw the beginning of the Wars of the Roses. Defeated in battle by supporters of Edward, son of Richard, the Duke of York — whose title to the throne, as a descendant of Edward III, was as strong as his own — Henry VI was brought a prisoner to the Tower in 1465, his gilt spurs struck off and his feet bound under his horse by leather thongs. A kind, studious, and retiring man, preoccupied with religious observances, Henry was not a difficult prisoner, and apparently he was not treated harshly. He was allowed visits from his friends, the use of his breviary, the company of his favorite bird and dog; but even with these comforts the years that he spent in confinement cannot have been other than miserable.

On the very night that his rival entered London in triumph as Edward IV — after a resounding victory over Henry's supporters at Tewkesbury in 1471 — Henry was found dead in his cell. It was given out that the king had died of "pure displeasure and melancholy"; but few doubted that the death of Henry's son, Prince Edward, at Tewkesbury had removed the last motive for keeping him alive and that he had been murdered.

During the reign of the usurper — the tall, handsome, autocratic, wonderfully energetic, and exuberantly sensual Edward IV — the Tower once more became one of the most pleasurable haunts of the court. It was an extremely gay court, although not an unduly extravagant one, for in *The Black Book of the Household*, which was issued in Edward's reign, the rights, duties, and stipulated perquisites of all the members of the royal household were carefully regulated.

The king's chamber in the Tower, as in all the royal palaces, was divided, both architecturally and by the constitution, into three sections. There was the outer or audience chamber, where the king held receptions; the inner or privy chamber, where he could talk more privately; and the bedchamber, where he could behave as he liked with his intimates. The attendants, who waited upon the king in these various chambers under the direction of the Lord Chamberlain, were classified into a strict hierarchy. There were the Knights for the Body,

highest ranking of the courtiers; the Squires for the Body, who slept in his room and helped him to dress and undress; the Squires for the Household, who served at table; the Gentlemen Ushers, who supervised the protocol; the Yeomen of the Crown, who were messengers; the Yeomen of the Chamber, who acted as torchbearers; the Grooms and Pages of the Chamber, young sons of noble families, sent to court to learn the ways and manners of the world and to perform various menial tasks — which even included making sure that the dogs did not dirty the floors.

Every royal activity was meticulously ordered. Twenty Squires for the Household were required to attend the king when he dined: a Server had to supervise the choreographic ceremonial of presenting the dishes; a Ewer had to be in attendance with a towel and a basin of water so that His Majesty could wash when he had eaten; a "Doctoure of Physyque" had to stand by his chair to advise him as to "which dyet is best according, and to the nature and operacion of all the metes"; thirteen minstrels had to play throughout the meal in the gallery; a jester had to make the king laugh when the meal was finished so that he could digest it the more satisfactorily.

The making of the bed in the king's bedchamber was subject to regulations quite as rigorous as those to be observed when he dined. Two Squires for the Body had to be present to stand at the head of the bed, while two Grooms of the Chamber stood at the foot. The Yeoman of the Chamber carried in the bedclothes, and a Gentleman Usher held back the curtains so that they could be placed upon the mattress. The method of laying down the sheets, of striking them down and smoothing them out, of laying on the cotton blanket and the ermine counterpane, of folding down the covers "the space of an ell," of beating the pillows and arranging them on the bed, of sprinkling holy water on the final product, was all described in the minutest detail.

Edward IV was not a man, however, to pay an unduly scrupulous attention to protocol; and court life at the Tower was informal enough in comparison with that led at other palaces in Europe. There were picnics on Tower Green to be enjoyed, trips on the river, games of bowls and archery, competitions on the Tower lawns. Sometimes there would be jousts and tournaments in Smithfield — the street in West Smithfield known today as Giltspur Street, and formerly as Knightrider Street, marks the route the courtiers took on their ride to the tourney ground from the Tower.

The new king got on well with the citizens of London, who readily succumbed to his charm and friendly *bonhomie.* A man of voracious sexual appetite, Edward had numerous mistresses, many of them — like the beautiful Jane Shore, wife of a Lombard Street goldsmith — the wives of London merchants. But it was not until the later years of his reign that his debaucheries and increasingly unscrupulous conduct turned the people of London against him. In 1478, Edward's wayward brother the Duke of Clarence, who had been plotting against the king, died in the Tower. The circumstances of his death were as mysterious as those in which Edward's other rival, Henry VI, had perished seven years earlier. Some said that the duke had been allowed to choose the form of a private death in place of a public execution; others, that he had died by accident. But the most persistent rumor that flew around London that

The portrait of RICHARD the 3. King of England, and Fraunce, Lord of Ireland. He was slaine at Boſworth feild. the 22ᵗʰ of Auguſt, 1486. and homelye buried at the Graye friers Church in Leiceſter, when he had vſurped 2 yeares 2 monthes and one day

winter was that Clarence had been drowned in a butt of Malmsey wine.

Five years later the Tower was the scene of another, deeper mystery. Edward IV died in 1483, and his thirteen-year-old son was proclaimed his successor. While awaiting his coronation, Edward V and his younger brother, Richard, Duke of York, were lodged in the Tower; their uncle Richard, Duke of Gloucester, was appointed to the office of Protector.

Richard is perhaps the most controversial figure in the whole of English history. To some historians he remains the monster that Shakespeare portrayed; to others — discrediting the later propaganda of those who defeated him, upon which the drama *Richard III* is based — he is a paragon. Certainly he was not the ill-featured hunchback of Shakespeare's description; nor was he guilty of many of the atrocious crimes with which he stood charged. But there can be no doubt that he was a man whose character was not out of tune with the ruthless spirit of the Renaissance. Although there is no precise evidence that he was responsible for the most notorious murders ever committed in the Tower, there is also no evidence that he was not.

The first of these murders was that of Lord Hastings, the young king's chamberlain, whose loyalty to Edward V was unquestioned and, therefore, to the protector, intolerable. According to Sir Thomas More, who had the story from the Bishop of Ely, an eyewitness, Hastings attended a meeting of the council in the Tower on June 14, 1483, at which the protector, in a furious rage, accused Jane Shore, his late brother's mistress, and Queen Elizabeth, his brother's wife, of sorcery. "See how by their witchcraft they have wasted my body," he shouted, pulling up his left doublet sleeve to his elbow to reveal an arm withered since his childhood.

"Certainly, my lord," replied Hastings, "if they have so heinously done, they be worthy of heinous punishment."

"And do you reply to me," exclaimed the protector, "with your ifs and your buts? You are the chief abettor of that witch Shore. You are yourself a traitor, and I swear by St. Paul that I will not dine before your head be brought."

He then struck the table with his fist. The guard rushed into the council chamber as though in obedience to a prearranged signal, and Hastings was dragged outside to the lawn in front of St. Peter's Chapel, where his neck was forced down onto a log and his head struck off with a poleaxe. Others of the protector's opponents on the council were thrown into the Tower dungeons; and three days later the protector had himself proclaimed King Richard III.

Shortly after his coronation, Richard set out upon a royal progress through the Midland counties to the north. It was while on this progress, again according to Sir Thomas More, that he dispatched a trusted messenger, John Green, to the Constable of the Tower, Sir Robert Brackenbury. Green carried instructions that the two royal children, the king's nephews, should be put to death. Brackenbury — to his credit — immediately refused, and Green reported the constable's refusal to the king at Warwick, "wherewith he took much displeasure and that same night said to a page of his, 'Ah! Whom shall a man trust?' "

The page recommended Sir James Tyrrell, Master of the Horse, a confirmed supporter of Richard and

one anxious to win his approval. Tyrrell and his brother at that moment were sleeping on a pallet outside the king's bedchamber. "Whereupon the King rose and came into the pallet chamber and said unto them merrily, 'What, sirs, be ye in bed so soon?' and calling Sir James Tyrrell up, brake to him secretly his mind in this mischievous matter. . . . Wherefore on the morrow he sent him to Brackenbury with a letter by which he was commanded to deliver to Sir James all the Keys of the Tower for a night."

Accompanied by his groom John Dighton, "a big, broad, square, strong knave," Sir James Tyrrell rode back to the Tower. There, in what was then known as Garden Tower, the two children were incarcerated, guarded by five rough jailers, all of their own attendants having been dismissed on the king's orders. They had also been deprived of all the privileges of royalty and were described as clinging to each other in terror, not troubling to tie the points of their shoes, crying for their mother and their dead father, "lingering in thought and heaviness till the traiterous deed delivered them from their wretchedness."

Tyrrell chose the hour of midnight for their murder and sent in Dighton and the most ruffianly of the jailers, Miles Forest, a "fellow fleshed in murder before," to kill them by smothering them with their pillows. When this had been done, Tyrrell was called in to see the bodies. "Satisfied of their death," More concludes, "he caused the murderers to bury them at the stairfoot, deep in the ground, under a great heap of stones."

Almost two centuries later, in the reign of Charles II (1660–85), the skeletons of two boys were found beneath a staircase in the White Tower. Certain that they must be the remains of the two murdered princes, Charles gave orders for the bones to be buried in Westminster Abbey in the Chapel of Henry VII.

Richard III did not live long to profit by his crime — if indeed the crime were his — for on August 22, 1485, he was defeated by a rival contender for the throne, Henry, Earl of Richmond, at the battle of Bosworth Field. It was the last battle of the Wars of the Roses. To consolidate his victory, and as a pledge to the country that the rivalry between their two families was over at last, Henry VII married Elizabeth of York, daughter of Edward IV, in January 1486.

Elizabeth was brought to the Tower — where her two brothers had so recently been murdered — in a barge "freshely furnished with banners and stremers of silk." She was accompanied by her mother and attended by the city authorities in a wonderful variety of other garlanded barges, at the helm of one of which an immense red dragon spouted fire into the Thames.

On the day of her coronation, "royally apparelled" in cloth of gold and damask and an ermine mantle, with her "yellow hair hanging downe playne byhynd her back," Elizabeth was carried to Westminster Abbey in a litter. There was a circlet of gold "richely garnyshed with precious Stonys upon her Hede"; and the crowds thronging the route and filling the roofs and windows, delighted by the beauty and freshness of their young queen, cheered her loudly as she passed.

All the streets between the Tower and the Abbey were decorated with banners and tapestries, and every now and again the royal procession would halt as a pageant was enacted in its honor or a choir began to sing. The Age of the Tudors had begun.

III

THE TUDOR PRISON

In the early summer of 1509, the royal household at the Tower began preparing "for so greate a celebration as had never before been seene." The king was to marry Catherine, daughter of Ferdinand and Isabella of Spain, and a great court was to be held at the Tower before their coronation.

Henry VIII was then eighteen. He was a magnificent youth, over six feet tall with the strength of an ox and the grace of a panther, yet the beauty of his round, cherubic face, despite a large and ill-shaped nose, would have become a pretty woman. He had the fair complexion, faint eyebrows, and auburn hair that his contemporaries so much admired. He was so "very beautiful," one foreign observer thought; another described him as "like a golden god."

The youthful monarch gave the impression of caring "for nothing but hunting and girls." Every day he was up early, riding, shooting, hawking, jousting, or wrestling. Every night he was up late dancing, leaping about to the music with exuberant enthusiasm. There seemed no end to his talents; he wore his companions out with his tireless energy. Nor was it true that he thought of nothing but exercise and sports and sensual delights. He could play the recorder, flute, or virginal with equal grace; he wrote anthems, he composed music; he was a scholar; he talked well. He was supremely accomplished, and inordinately self-confident.

The royal household awaited Henry's arrival at the Tower from Greenwich with some trepidation. At Greenwich, since it was not yet the season for hunting or hawking, the courtiers had been commanded to "eschew idleness" by playing at "barriers," a new contest in which the combatants, wearing special breastplates and helmets, fought each other with seven-foot-long lances and two-headed swords. There were also regular jousts and tournaments and games of running at the ring. In the evenings there were dances and feasts, revelries and masquerades. It was clear that the festivities at the Tower would be very exhausting for almost everyone except the king, always "the most assiduous *and the most interested.*"

As it happened, all went well. The entire elaborate household was in attendance; and cloth of scarlet and red, white, and green, festooned the chambers. The king was served at dinner by processions of courtiers, whom he had chosen to honor as Knights of the Bath, an ancient order of knighthood particularly associated with the Tower. Tradition demanded that aspirants to the order should take ritual ablutions in tubs in a room adjoining the Chapel of St. John in the White Tower, and then, after dining with the king, keep an all-night vigil in the candlelit chapel with their armor laid before the altar.

On June 23, 1509, Henry and Catherine left the Tower for their coronation — he, splendidly clothed in crimson velvet furred with ermine, and shining with rubies, emeralds, and diamonds; she, in a litter between two white palfreys, dressed more simply in white satin, with her auburn hair, "of very great length, beautiful and goodly to behold," flowing down her back.

In the ensuing years, the king returned to the Tower from time to time, noting with satisfaction the gradual improvements being made to the structure. In 1520, work on the charming new Chapel of St. Peter ad Vincula was completed. The previous chapel, consecrated in the reign of William the Conqueror's son,

Henry I, and rebuilt at the end of the thirteenth century, had been almost completely destroyed by fire in 1512. Ten years after the new chapel was finished, a large building was put up in the inner ward to serve as lodgings for the lieutenant, the officer responsible for the defense and maintenance of the Tower in the name of the constable. Two years after that, the uncompromising starkness of St. Thomas's Tower — the principal tower facing the river — was alleviated by timber framing. The stark appearance of the White Tower was also softened when the flat, embattled tops of the four turrets were embellished with decorative caps.

By the time these early sixteenth-century improvements had been carried out, however, the Tower was no longer the king's principal residence in London. For after the fall from power in 1529 of Cardinal Wolsey, Henry's chief minister, both Hampton Court — the cardinal's Thames-side palace outside London — and York Place — his fine town residence as Archbishop of York — were taken into royal ownership. York Place, splendid as it already was, was much improved and extended; renamed Whitehall Palace, it became the king's most magnificent palace in London.

Thereafter the royal apartments at the Tower were only occasionally opened for brief visits by the court. The famous fortress, henceforth, was used mainly as a state prison. Some parts of the Tower, of course, had always been used as a prison. Indeed, one of the earliest prisoners was Rannulf Flambard, Bishop of Durham, William Rufus's chief minister and the man responsible for various improvements to the Tower after its presumed architect, Gundulf, had moved to Rochester. Rannulf had been held in the White Tower on the

Es nouuelles dalbion
Il vous en plaist escouter
Mon frere z mon copuignio

orders of Henry I for having "stopped all justice" in
the previous reign when "money was lord."

The names of Rannulf's successors as prisoners in
the Tower sound like a roll call of the great and infamous names of medieval Europe. Kings and princes,
archbishops and abbots, queens and murderesses, traitors and saints, freebooters and counterfeiters, had all
been held captive within its walls. The kings of Scotland and France had been held there for ransom after
their defeats in battle. Griffin, eldest son of Llewelyn,
Prince of Wales, had been deprived of his birthright
in the reign of Henry III and was held for four years.

In the reign of Henry III's son, Edward I, King
Baliol of Scotland and numerous Scottish noblemen
had been incarcerated after their defeat at Dunbar in
1296. Also imprisoned during these years were the
Grand Master of the Knights Templar and all the
English knights of the order who had been accused of
a fantastic variety of unnatural and vicious practices.
Later on in the fourteenth century scores more Scottish
prisoners had appeared, including their king, David
Bruce, captured after the battle of Neville's Cross in
1346 and escorted to the Tower by an armed body of
20,000 men. Bruce was forced to ride a high black
charger, to make him the more conspicuous, through
streets lined with spectators and with the City companies in their finest liveries drawn up to watch the
passing of their country's humiliated enemy.

No sooner had Bruce been ransomed than the
Tower had again been filled, this time with Welsh
prisoners captured in the battles along the Marches
and with French prisoners captured at Poitiers in 1356.
Among these last was John, King of France, who was

not released until 1360, when the treaty of Brétigny
and the payment of three million crowns ransom at
last permitted him to return home. A new generation
of French prisoners appeared in 1415 after the battle
of Agincourt — fought during the painfully contracted
Hundred Years' War with France — including the
counts of Richemont, Eu, and Vendôme, the dukes of
Orléans and Bourbon, and Jean Bouciquaut, Marshal
of France. Bouciquaut and Bourbon died in captivity,
unable to pay the heavy ransoms Henry V demanded
for them. The Count of Vendôme remained a prisoner
until 1423; the Count of Eu, until 1425. The Duke of
Orléans, who wrote many of his poems in the White
Tower, was not released until 1440, when his huge
ransom was at last paid.

Although the Tower had held a great number and
variety of prisoners in the five centuries since its
construction, in no reign previous to that of Henry
VIII had its walls enclosed so many English opponents
of the royal will. Nor in previous reigns had most
prisoners been treated badly. The French, Scottish, and
Welsh prisoners of war certainly were not; nor was the
nine-year-old Prince James of Scotland — later King
James I (1424–37) — who was brought to the Tower after the ship taking him to France was intercepted off
the Yorkshire coast; nor was Margaret of Anjou, queen
consort of Henry VI, who was confined there after her
husband's murder; nor were rich prisoners like William
de la Pole, Duke of Suffolk, John de Vere, Earl of
Oxford, and other disgraced ministers, fallen favorites,
and traitorous nobles for whom confinement meant
little worse than the deprivation of liberty. In fact, like
Rannulf Flambard, the first prisoner of whom there is

record, prisoners were usually permitted to keep an excellent table for themselves and their servants, and to enjoy most of the comforts that had given them pleasure in the days of their freedom.

There were exceptions, of course. William de Marescis, the wellborn leader of a gang of freebooters that had terrified the people of the western coasts of England for several years in the reign of Henry III, was confined with irons in the deepest and darkest of the Tower's dungeons before his execution. And Sir Henry Wyatt, an impoverished Lancastrian knight who had been captured during one of the fierce battles of the Wars of the Roses, had been incarcerated in a damp, cold dungeon without fire, bed, or even food. One day, it is reported, "a cat came down into the dungeon with him, and as it were, offered herself unto him. He was glad of her, laid her on his bosom to warm him, and by making much of her, won her love. After this she would come every day unto him divers times, and, when she could get one, bring him a pigeon." Previously Wyatt had extracted a promise from the jailer that in the unlikely event of his finding food it would be cooked for him. The jailer kept his word, and Wyatt contrived to remain alive until a change in the fortunes of the war brought about his release.

It was not until the Reformation brought the first of Henry VIII's victims to the Tower that the harsh treatment of prisoners became almost a matter of policy. One of the earliest of these victims was John Fisher, Bishop of Rochester, whose conscience would not allow him to accept either the doctrine of royal supremacy or the validity of Henry VIII's divorce from Catherine of Aragon in 1533.

Fisher was confined in conditions of piteous indignity. "I byseche you to be goode, master, unto me in my necessitie," he implored Thomas Cromwell, the Lord Great Chamberlain, "for I have neither shirt nor sute, nor yet other clothes that are necessary for me to wear, but that bee ragged and rent so shamefullie. Notwithstanding, I might easily suffer that, if they would keep my body warm." But he could not keep warm, nor could he eat the meager portions of unpalatable food that were provided for him. He was an old man of seventy-four, he pleaded, and of a delicate constitution; unless he were allowed the sort of food to which his "slender dyett" had made him accustomed, he would "decay forthwith." In his reply, Cromwell dismissed his pleas as "mere craft and cunning"; yet one of the few visitors Fisher was permitted to see, the Bishop of Coventry and Lichfield, described him as "near gone" and "unable to bear the clothes on his back."

Neither Cromwell nor his master, Henry VIII, could be persuaded to show the good and gentle old man the least mercy. When Pope Paul III made Fisher a cardinal, his death was decided upon. On June 17, 1535, he was pronounced guilty of treason and sentenced to a traitor's death. "Your sentence," the court's dreaded formula ran, "is that you be led back to prison; laid on a hurdle, and so drawn to the place of execution; there to be hanged, to be cut down alive, your privy members cut off and cast into the fire, your bowels burnt before your eyes, your head smitten off, your body quartered and divided at the King's will. God have mercy on your soul. Amen!"

It was fixed that the place of punishment for Bishop Fisher should be Tower Hill, an open space beyond the northwest angle of the Tower's moat, which had long been recognized as the traitors' execution ground, and there a scaffold was erected.

Early in the morning of the day on which he was to die, Fisher took off the hair shirt he had been wearing in his cell and dressed himself in the clean clothes that had at last been provided for him. When the lieutenant arrived to take him away he carefully wrapped a fur cape around his shoulders. "Oh, my Lord!" the lieutenant said. "What need you be so careful of your health for this little time?" But Fisher was weak and ill and he felt the cold. He did not want people to see him shiver and think he was afraid.

He picked up his Latin Bible, made the sign of the cross, and followed the lieutenant down the stone steps. Scarcely able to reach the bottom, he was then placed in a chair and carried to the gate of the Middle Tower to await the arrival of the sheriffs. While waiting there he got out of the chair and, leaning against the walls of the gateway, raised up his Bible and said, "Oh Lord, this is the last time that I shall ever open this book, let some comfortable place now chance to me, whereby I, Thy poor servant, may glorify Thee in this my last hour." The book fell open at the passage: "I have glorified Thee on the earth, I have finished the work which Thou gavest me to do. And now, O Father, glorify Thou me with Thine own self."

"Here," said Fisher earnestly, "is learning enough for me to my life's end." He returned to the chair and was carried to the scaffold. He climbed the steps unaided and replied to the executioner who knelt before him, as was customary, to ask for his forgiveness: "I forgive thee with all my heart, and I trust thou shalt see me overcome this storm with courage."

Asking the crowd to pray for him, Fisher declared that he had come to die for the faith of Christ's Holy Catholic Church. He prayed for the king and for the happiness of the country. Then he knelt down on the straw around the block and repeated the Te Deum and Psalm 31. The barbaric preliminaries of his sentence had been commuted, and he had only to face the axe. He gave the customary sign that he was ready for it by stretching out his arms. It fell, and his head was severed in a single stroke.

The executioner held Fisher's head up to the crowd, repeating the traditional formula, "So perish all the King's enemies. Behold the head of a traitor." Then the people rushed forward — as they always did upon such occasions — to dip their handkerchiefs in the blood splashed upon the scaffold and dripping between the planks. They also snatched up pieces of blood-stained straw as mementos, relics, and curatives; for the blood of men thus executed was considered a remedy for all manner of ills.

Fisher's body was left on the scaffold until evening, when it was taken to the churchyard of All Hallows Barking-by-the-Tower before being buried in the recently completed Chapel of St. Peter ad Vincula within the Tower's walls. His head was parboiled and displayed — as the heads of traitors commonly were — on a pole on London Bridge. But so many people crowded around to look upon Fisher's head with reverence — some even declaring that it grew "fresher and more comely day by day" — that "almost neither horse nor cart could pass over the Bridge," and it soon had to be removed by the authorities.

A fortnight later Fisher's friend, the noble Sir Thomas More, once Henry VIII's Lord Chancellor, who had also incurred the wrath of his master by refusing to take the Oath of Supremacy, followed him to the scaffold.

At first Sir Thomas was treated well enough in the Tower. As a knight his fees were only ten shillings a week for himself and five shillings for his servant, and his wife was actually compelled to sell some of her clothes to pay them. But the money was found, and More was provided with decent clothing and enough to eat. He was allowed to receive visitors as often as he cared to, and he enjoyed the use of his books. But when he remained obdurate in his refusal to countenance the king's right to the title of Supreme Head of the Church, both his books and his writing materials were taken away from him, and his own servant was replaced by another who could neither read nor write. Using a piece of coal, More contrived to write a letter to his beloved daughter, Margaret, to assure her that her "tender, loving father" forgot neither her nor any of his family and friends in his "pore prayers"; but he spent most of the time in the dark, with the shutters of his cell firmly closed.

On July 1, 1535, Sir Thomas More was indicted of high treason at Westminster Hall and condemned, like Fisher, to a traitor's death. He returned to the Tower by barge, and as he alighted on Tower Wharf, Margaret was there to say good-by to him and receive his blessing. She burst into tears when she saw him, pushed her way through the guards surrounding him, and threw her arms around his neck. The guards pulled her away gently, moved by her distress, but she ran back to her father again, enclosing him once more in her arms. She tried to speak to him, yet all she could say through her sobs was, "Oh, my father, Oh, my father." He blessed her, kissed her, and moved on.

As in Fisher's case, the king commuted the ghastly sentence for treason to a simple beheading and graciously granted permission for More's family to attend the ceremony — a favor that More wryly hoped would not be granted to his friends. He was informed on July 6 that he was to die that very morning. With all the composure that Fisher had displayed, he came out to execution wearing a coarse peasant coat and carrying a red cross. "I pray thee see me safely up," he said to the lieutenant at the bottom of the steps, "but as for my coming down again, let me shift for myself."

He tipped the scarlet uniformed headsman, and as lightheartedly as he had spoken to the lieutenant, he said to him, "You will never get any credit for beheading me, my neck is so short." And when he had knelt down at the block, he added, "Let me lay my beard over the block lest you cut it, for *it* has never committed treason." He died, he said, for the faith of the Catholic Church. He remained the king's faithful servant, but he was God's servant first.

The incarceration and execution of Fisher and More in the Tower foreshadowed the imprisonment and death of many others who came between Henry VIII and his tyrannical will. One of the first of these was Anne Boleyn, for the love of whom the king had divorced Catherine of Aragon.

Anne was a swarthy, flat-chested young woman, yet witty, provocative, exciting, and excitable. From the beginning Henry — captivated by Anne's vivacity, her

dark, flashing eyes, her long, loose black hair — had found her irresistible. He married her on a winter's morning in 1533, when she was already pregnant with his child. Before long, however, he grew tired of Anne, irritated by her hectic tantrums and impatient of her apparent inability to bear him a son. And he had fallen in love with someone else — a small, fair, demure girl, Jane Seymour, whom he boldly appointed lady-in-waiting to the queen.

One day Queen Anne came into her antechamber and found Jane Seymour sitting on her husband's knee. She flew into one of her by-then familiar tantrums, became hysterical, tore a locket the king had given Jane from her rival's neck, cutting her hand badly. Soon afterward Anne gave birth, prematurely, to a stillborn son. Her husband never forgave her.

Three months later during a joust at Greenwich, Anne dropped her handkerchief. Henry — affecting to believe that she had done so as a sign of encouragement to an illicit lover — stormed from the field, returned to Westminster, and there gave orders for the arrest of the queen on charges of treason, adultery, and incest.

Also charged with Anne, and thrown with her into the Tower, were five men accused of having been her lovers. One of these was her brother George, Lord Rochford, whom she was said to have allured "with her tongue in the said George's mouth and the said George's tongue in hers." A sixth man, the poet Sir Thomas Wyatt, was also later sent to the Tower, accused of adultery with the queen.

Wyatt and the others all denied the charges. But one of them, a young musician named Mark Smeaton, "one of the prettiest monochord players and deftest dancers in the land,'' was taken down to the Tower's torture chamber for questioning.

It was held against Smeaton that he was performing on the monochord one day when the queen remarked, "Does not the lad play well?" Afterwards, her accusers said, she had gone into a stillroom where candied fruits were stored and had asked her servant Margaret to bring her some marmalade. "Here is the marmalade, my lady," Margaret had said, pushing the trembling Smeaton toward her. The queen had grabbed him and taken him to bed where he had "soon lost his bashfulness. . . . He remained that night and many others."

At first the musician denied the truth of the story. But in the torture chamber a knotted rope was twisted around his head with a cudgel, and Smeaton soon admitted that he had, in fact, "violated" the queen three times. But Smeaton had never been in her room, except once at Winchester, the queen insisted. She could never have made love to him; he was the worst-dressed man in the palace; he wore no jeans; he was no gentleman. She collapsed in hysterics.

"Shall I go into a dungeon?" the queen asked Sir William Kingston, the Constable of the Tower, upon her arrival at the fortress. "No, madame," he replied. "You shall go into your lodging that you lay in at your coronation."

"Jesus have mercy upon me," she said. Then she "kneeled down, weeping apace," Kingston reported to Thomas Cromwell, "and in the same sorrow fell into a great laughing, which she hath done several times since. . . . And then she said, 'Mr. Kingston, do you know wherefore I am here?' and I said, 'Nay'; and then she asked me, 'When saw you the King?' and I said, 'I saw

Henry VIII (1509-1547)

1. Catherine of Aragon —— Mary (1553-1558)
   —divorced
2. Anne Boleyn —— Elizabeth I (1558-1603)
   —beheaded
3. Jane Seymour —— Edward VI (1547-1553)
   —died in childbed
4. Anne of Cleves
   —divorced
5. Catherine Howard
   —beheaded
6. Catherine Parr
   —survived

him not since I saw him yesterday in the Tilt Yard.' And then said she, 'I pray you to tell me where my father is?' And I told her I saw him before dinner in the Court. 'And where is my sweet brother?' And I said I left him at York Place [Whitehall Palace], and so I did. 'I hear say,' said she, 'that I shall be accused with three men, and I can say no more than nay, without I should open my body,' and therewith opened her gown. Then she said, 'Mr. Kingston, shall I die without justice?' And I said, 'The poorest subject the King hath hath justice,' and therewith she laughed."

Anne Boleyn's spirits soon recovered. She persuaded herself that the king was keeping her in the Tower to test her; he would soon let her out again. The next day she grew quite "merry," and "made a great dinner." But then, the constable said, she fell into hysterics again, and laughed and laughed — and could not stop laughing.

Kingston was ordered to keep close watch upon the queen, to make a note of anything she might say that could be used in evidence against her, to "charge the gentlewomen that waited upon the Queen that they should have no communication with her," unless his wife were present. However, "it cannot be so," he reported, "for my Lady Boleyn [Anne's sister-in-law] and Mistress Cofyn lie on the Queen's pallet, and I and my wife at the door without; and they can talk inside without us hearing them. But I have everything told me by Mistress Cofyn."

On May 15, 1536, the queen was brought to trial in the Tower's council chamber above the Lieutenant's Lodgings. Both her father, Thomas Boleyn, Earl of Wiltshire — who could not bring himself to speak —

and her uncle, the Duke of Norfolk, were members of the court of twenty-six peers that had been assembled to try her. Her brother, Lord Rochford, stood in the dock beside her. The other accused men had already been tried in Westminster Hall and condemned to death. Although Anne's guilt seemed thus to have been decided, Anne herself was composed, calm, collected. She seemed, indeed, "unmoved as a stock," conducting herself throughout with the "bearing of one coming to great honour."

Cogently and convincingly she denied each charge as it was put to her: she had never been other than faithful to her lord; she had never taken to bed any of the men accused with her. Her brother was equally firm and convincing, so convincing that men said that even Sir Thomas More had not acquitted himself better, that surely he would not be found guilty on the evidence submitted. All that appeared to have been proved against him was that he had once, in company, leaned over his sister's bed.

But men reckoned without the king, whose mind was implacably made up. Both Rochford and Anne were condemned to death by the unanimous verdict of the peers. Rochford was to die by beheading. Anne was to die either by being burned as a witch or also by beheading, whichever was the "King's pleasure."

As soon as she heard the verdict, Anne leaped to her feet in the council chamber protesting her innocence. "O Father! O Creator!" she cried out. "Thou knowest that I have not deserved this death."

She steadfastly refused to believe that the king would insist upon her execution. He would let her die in exile in Hanover, or at least allow her to retire into a nunnery. Even when her brother was beheaded, the queen still insisted to her ladies that she would never be made to suffer his fate. "The King does this to prove me," she protested; he would certainly pardon her at the last minute.

In the end Sir William persuaded her otherwise. The scaffold was all prepared on Tower Green — within the walls of the Tower, so that she would have more privacy than she could have expected on Tower Hill. She could even see the scaffold from the windows of her room. She was to mount it on the morning of May 19. Toward the middle of that morning when no summons had yet come, Anne sent for Sir William, and said to him, "Mr. Kingston, I hear say, I shall not die before noon, and I am very sorry therefore, for I thought to be dead now and past my pain." "I told her it should be no pain, it was so subtle," Sir William wrote to Cromwell. "Then she said, 'I have heard say that the executioner is very good, and I have a very little neck'; and putting her hands about it laughed heartily."

It was Anne's last display of hysterics. Thereafter, she seemed quite resigned to her death. Indeed, as Kingston recorded, at the end she seemed almost to welcome it. "I have seen many men, and also women executed, and they have been in great sorrow, but, to my knowledge, this lady has much joy and pleasure in death. Her almoner is continually with her, and has been today since two of the clock after midnight."

Anne wrote to her husband that last night, once again protesting her innocence and acknowledging the many favors she had received at his hands. She begged him to take her baby daughter, the Princess Elizabeth, into his paternal care.

At last the summons came, and Anne Boleyn slowly walked out across Tower Green toward the scaffold, followed by four of her ladies. "Looking frequently behind her," she climbed the scaffold, which had been raised higher than was usual so that the few privileged spectators could have a good view of her death. She made a short speech to them, addressing them as "Good Christian people," and assured them that she had come hither to die according to the law and that she "had nothing against it." She praised the king's mercy, a customary hypocrisy, since the victim thereby hoped to protect his relatives and dependents — "for a gentler nor a more merciful prince was there never." "I take my leave of you and the world," she concluded, "and I heartily desire you all to pray for me."

One of Anne's ladies helped her off with her ermine-trimmed cloak, and then Anne herself took off her white hood and put on in its place a white linen cap into which she could tuck her long hair. Then her eyes were bandaged. She looked so beautiful, calm, and innocent that for a moment it seemed as if the executioner would be unable to perform his task. He was a Frenchman, especially brought over from St. Omer because of his great skill in wielding a sword and slicing through a neck in an instant. He had no need of a block. Anne knelt down resignedly before him, arranging her skirts so that her ankles and feet were covered. The headsman picked up his sword, which had been concealed from view beneath a pile of straw. With the weapon in his hands, he pretended to walk away to the scaffold steps calling out, "Bring me the sword!" Anne instinctively turned her bandaged eyes to look toward him, and before the queen realized what was happen-

The perpetual intrigues and gross sensuality that marked Henry VIII's reign eventually marked the high-handed, high-living monarch's face as well. In the 1544 engraving at right, Henry appears porcine, glowering, and fully capable of ordering the execution of such diverse "opponents" as Catherine Howard, his fifth queen (right center); Chamberlain Thomas Cromwell (far right); and the arrogant but guileless Earl of Surrey, who dared to assert his claim to the throne by adding the royal lions to his coat of arms (right below).

ing, the headsman struck down and killed her.

One of Anne Boleyn's accusers, Thomas Cromwell, did not long survive the queen. The brilliant administrator had outlived his usefulness and had made too many enemies. Friendless and forsaken, Cromwell was dispatched to the Tower on June 10, 1540. He was accused of high treason, but in fact was guilty of no worse offense than hubris, ruthlessness in the royal service, and what was unforgivable in Henry's eyes — and in the eyes of Cromwell's powerful enemy, the Duke of Norfolk — advocacy of the king's marriage to the plain and uninteresting German Protestant princess Anne of Cleves. The king's third wife, Jane Seymour, had died in childbed in 1537.

From the Tower Cromwell wrote frantically to the king, appealing for "mercye, mercye, mercye." As though struck by the repetition of the word with which it ended, Henry had the letter read over to him three times, but he did not answer it. And on the very day that his faithful servant was beheaded at Tyburn, the king — after Anne of Cleves had been happily divorced — married his fifth wife, Catherine Howard. Henry believed that in Catherine he had obtained "a jewel of womanhood" who loved him with "perfect love."

Catherine Howard was as vivacious as Anne, yet less intelligent. She was short, rather fat, and twenty-one; the king was forty-nine. Soon, however, Catherine was found to be as imperfect a jewel as had been her cousin, Anne Boleyn.

At first Henry refused to believe the charges that were brought against his new queen. When Archbishop Cranmer handed him a letter that accused Catherine of having lived "most corruptly and sensually,"

he dismissed it as a forgery. He had a "constant opinion" of his young wife's character and devotion to him, and he declined to give any credit to what he ascribed to malicious gossip. But then her former lovers were arrested and questioned, and a scandalous history began to emerge. It appeared that Catherine, while living in the household of her grandmother, the Duchess of Norfolk, had often allowed her music master, Henry Mannock, to "feel the secrets and other parts" of her body. Later her kinsman Francis Dereham had actually "known her carnally many times, both in his doublet and hose between the sheets and in naked bed." Since her marriage, her accusers said, she and her cousin, Thomas Culpepper, had frequently spent many hours together in her room at night.

The king was appalled by these accusations. At first he sat "pierced with pensiveness." Then, calling for a sword, he swore that the queen would never have as much "delight in her inconstancy as she should have torture in her death." Finally, to the consternation of his council, he burst into tears. Later on, more characteristically, Henry blamed the council for "this last mischief."

The queen at first denied all the charges, then hysterically confessed that before her marriage Mannock had indeed handled and touched the secret parts of her body, and that Francis Dereham had lain with her naked and had used her "in such a sort as a man doth his wife many and sundry times." But she vehemently denied that Thomas Culpepper had ever done such things after her marriage, although she agreed that she had called him her "little sweet fool" and had given him a present of a cap and a ring. Nor, even under

torture in the Tower, would Culpepper admit that he had lain with the queen; yet the very fact that it was known that he had wanted to do so was enough to secure his conviction. Dereham also denied under torture that he had lain with the queen since her marriage; yet the very fact that he had been appointed her secretary was enough for the court to presume their evil intention and malice, and therefore to condemn him to death for high treason.

Culpepper and Dereham were both held in the Tower pending their execution. Indeed, the Tower had become so clogged with prisoners involved in the queen's disgrace that the lieutenant was obliged to ask the king if the royal apartments might be used as prison cells. If so, would he lend the lieutenant his "double key." The king did not remember that he had ever had a double key, but he gave the lieutenant permission to open the royal apartments and ordered the locks changed. Even so, not all of the accused could be accommodated in the Tower and cells for many of them had to be found in the ordinary criminal prisons of London.

Lady Rochford, Anne Boleyn's sister-in-law and a lady of the queen's privy chamber, had foolishly involved herself in the Culpepper affair; brought to the Tower, she went out of her mind during her lengthy, repetitive, and exhausting interrogation. Catherine's uncle, Lord William Howard, was imprisoned (her mother and father were dead). Also brought to the Tower were Catherine's aunt, Margaret, Lord William's wife; her brother Henry's wife; her aunt, Lady Bridgewater; and her cantankerous old grandmother, the dowager duchess, who complained crossly of the cold and discomforts of the Tower. She could not live in it, the old lady protested, and she asked for more consideration to be shown to her age and noble birth. Henry, to whom the request was referred, immediately denied it.

Catherine herself, a lonely, frightened figure, haughty and disdainful when not in hysterics, was conducted to the Tower in February 1542. She struggled when she saw the covered barge waiting at the river steps, and she had to be dragged into it. The barge was rowed downstream preceded by the galley of the Lord Privy Seal, with whom sat other members of the council; it was followed by the Duke of Suffolk in a barge crowded with guards and soldiers. As the little flotilla passed beneath Tower Bridge, the heads of Francis Dereham and Thomas Culpepper could be seen impaled upon their spikes.

By the time the vessels reached Tower Wharf, the queen had regained her composure. Dressed in black velvet, she stepped out of the barge and quietly walked up the steps to her cell.

Frivolous and inconsiderate as she had been as queen, Catherine Howard remained a brave and dignified prisoner throughout the time of her duress. When she was told, on the evening of February 12, 1542, that she was to die on the following day, she asked that the block be brought to her so that she might learn how to place herself with dignity. Her request was granted, and in her cell she practiced lying down and placing her neck on the groove in the block that had been especially made for her. At the end of her macabre rehearsal she expressed herself satisfied that she could conduct herself like a queen. And so she did.

The next morning at seven o'clock all the members of the council arrived at the Tower, with the exception of the Duke of Suffolk, who was ill, and her uncle, the Duke of Norfolk, who had wisely left the country until his family's disgrace should be forgotten. They watched Catherine walk to the scaffold, erected on the same spot on Tower Green as had been the one built for the execution of her predecessor, Anne Boleyn, six years earlier; and they noted how calm and collected she appeared. She was very weak and had to be helped up the steps. She even had difficulty in raising her voice to make the short speech and customary confession that was expected of her. But she made the "most godly and Christian end that ever was heard tell of."

So, too, did Lady Rochford, who immediately followed her onto the scaffold. Lady Rochford was still suffering from the effects of her recent mental breakdown and spent an unconscionable time enumerating the "several faults she had committed in her life"; but at the last she bore "a steadfast countenance" and "desired all Christian people" to take regard of her "worthy and just punishment."

On her last night Catherine had begged that her family should not be punished for her sins, and this desire, at least, was posthumously granted her. All her relations, together with their servants, were released from the Tower after the queen's death, and her uncle, the Duke of Norfolk, was allowed to return from his voluntary exile and was even received back into the king's favor.

Norfolk did not remain there for long. Other men, jealous of the Howards' power, had now ingratiated themselves with the king. Notable among them was

Catherine Howard, Henry's venal and vacuous fifth wife, spent the eve of her execution practicing — so that when she was led to the block (above) she would know how to conduct herself in a manner befitting her station.

Triggered by a directive from the Archbishop of Canterbury, a wave of iconoclasm swept England during the winter of 1548. In its wake a number of antipapal paintings were produced, among them this view of the dying Henry VIII, who is shown attended by black-robed ministers and gesturing toward his son and heir, Edward. The small inset at upper right depicts the boy-king's soldiers smashing images of the Catholic saints. A vanquished pope and two anguished friars slump at the feet of the new Protestant ruler.

Edward Seymour, Earl of Hertford, Jane Seymour's brother and uncle to Prince Edward, the king's son by her. Looking for an opportunity to bring his rival down, Hertford found it in the behavior of Norfolk's son, the Earl of Surrey.

Surrey was a clever young man, a brave soldier, and an accomplished poet. But he was fatally indiscreet and undisguisedly ambitious. Knowing that King Henry had not now long to live and wishing to draw attention to his claim to be descended from Edward the Confessor, Surrey amended his coat-of-arms so that the royal arms were given pride of place in the first quarter.

Nothing could have alarmed Henry more. Earlier in his reign he had had Edmund de la Pole, Earl of Suffolk and a nephew of Edward IV, hastily executed when he came to fear that the earl had pretensions to succeed him. He had also contrived the execution of Edward, third Duke of Buckingham, a direct descendant of Edward III. He had even countenanced the execution of Margaret Pole, Countess of Salisbury, daughter of the Duke of Clarence and niece of Edward IV, although she was nearly seventy. The proud woman had refused to put her gray head on the block as that was what traitors did. She had so shaken it from side to side — as though inviting the executioner to get it off as best he could — that her neck and shoulders were hideously hacked about before the decapitation was accomplished.

Having rid himself of these three troublesome connections from the former dynasty, Henry was not likely to have any compunction in disposing of the Earl of Surrey. And when Surrey began openly to advocate his father's right to become regent upon the king's death, the young man's fate was sealed.

Shortly before Christmas, Surrey and his father were arrested and thrown into the Tower. Surrey conducted his own defense with great skill and ingenuity, but a note from the king was enough to bring in a verdict of guilty and a sentence of "simple decapitation on Tower Hill within a week." His father was also condemned to death and his execution fixed for the morning of January 2, 1547.

The night before Norfolk's scheduled execution, it had become obvious to the king's attendants that Henry — now married to his sixth and last wife, Catherine Parr — was dying. No one dared to tell him so, for it was high treason to prophesy the king's death. But then Sir Anthony Denny, Groom of the Stole, plucked up courage and told Henry that in "man's judgement" he was "not like to live." Henry declined to believe it. On being asked if he wanted to see a priest, he replied that he had no need of one yet. He would take a little sleep. When he awoke it was nearly midnight, and he could not speak. He died at two o'clock in the morning.

The Duke of Norfolk, waiting for the time of his own death in the Tower a few hours later, was saved by the toll of the bell mourning Henry's death.

IV

THE SHADOW OF THE AXE

Within an hour of King Henry's death Lord Hertford left London for Ashridge in Hertfordshire to tell his nephew Prince Edward that he was king. Edward was then nine years old. When he heard the news from his uncle, who knelt before him to impart it, he burst into tears and clung to his half sister Elizabeth for comfort. The next morning Edward was taken to the Tower, and he remained in the royal apartments there, according to custom, until the day of his coronation.

No one outside the Tower saw the little boy again until, on the afternoon of February 19, 1547, he came out of the gateway of the Middle Tower wearing a gold-embroidered gown of silver cloth and a velvet cap thickly set with diamonds and pearls. Edward's horse, caparisoned in crimson satin sewn with pearls and gold damask, stood waiting for him under a canopy carried by six mounted noblemen. He rode to Westminster with his uncle Hertford (who had just been named Duke of Somerset and Lord Protector of the realm) on his left.

The Duke of Somerset did not live long to enjoy his new-found power. But before he was brought down, he successfully rid himself of his handsome, wayward, unscrupulous younger brother Thomas, Lord Seymour of Sudely. Seymour had married King Henry's widow, Catherine Parr, and after her death in childbed, had dared to make the most outrageous advances to the sixteen-year-old Princess Elizabeth. For such audacity, Seymour was executed on Tower Hill on the morning of March 20, 1549.

Although well-liked by the people, the Duke of Somerset was unable to withstand the ambitions of a powerful group of men that collected around John

Dudley, the Earl of Warwick and Duke of Northumberland. Accused by Northumberland and his followers in the council not only of plotting to seize the Tower and destroy London, but also of endeavoring to secure for himself and his heirs the succession to the crown, Somerset was thrown into the Tower and was himself beheaded on Tower Hill on January 22, 1552. The duke died bravely, protesting his innocence to the sympathetic spectators in a lengthy speech; he then knelt down calmly in the straw, with a handkerchief held to his eyes. He repeated the words "Lord Jesus, save me!" twice; as he began to say them for the third time, the axe fell. Somerset was buried in the Chapel of St. Peter ad Vincula above the bodies of Anne Boleyn and Catherine Howard.

By 1553, after six years of rule, the young king was seriously ill, and it soon became clear that Edward VI had not long to live. The Duke of Northumberland, having wrested power from Somerset, was determined not to lose it upon Edward's death. He conceived a plan to transfer the crown from the Tudors to his own family, the Dudleys. His first step was to arrange for his son, Lord Guildford Dudley, to marry the king's cousin, Lady Jane Grey, the fifteen-year-old daughter of Henry Grey, Duke of Suffolk, and granddaughter of a younger sister of Henry VIII. Northumberland's second step was to persuade Edward VI to nominate Lady Jane as his successor in place of his elder half sister, Princess Mary, the Roman Catholic daughter of Henry VIII by his first wife, Catherine of Aragon.

Dying of tuberculosis of the lungs, Edward VI agreed in the late spring of 1553 to nominate Lady Jane as his heir for the sake of the Protestant succession. On the afternoon of July 6 he died, poisoned by the medicine that his physician had prescribed, his limbs swollen, his skin darkened, his fingers and toes gangrenous, his hair and nails fallen out — a pathetic figure too weak to cough.

Although she fainted when told of her accession and then tearfully declared that she had no right to the crown since Princess Mary was the "rightful heir," Lady Jane eventually submitted to the entreaties of her relations and to what she took to be the will of God. Two days after the death of her cousin Edward had been announced, she was conducted to the Tower as the new reigning sovereign.

For her ceremonial entrance into the Tower, Lady Jane Grey was dressed in a richly brocaded gown and a long-sleeved white and green bodice embroidered with gold; the white coif on her head was studded with precious stones. Concealed beneath her skirts she wore wooden clogs with soles three inches thick, for the girl was so short that without them the silently watching crowds would never have been able to see her. Even with the clogs, Lady Jane presented a far from imposing figure as she stepped out of her barge onto Tower Wharf and walked toward the river gate. She advanced under a canopy supported by six noblemen, with her mother holding her train. A Genoese merchant noticed how thin the new monarch was, and how freckled the skin beneath the auburn hair. But she "is graceful and well made," he thought; "and when she smiled she showed her teeth which are white and sharp. In all she is a charming person, *graziosa e animata*." Her young husband walked by her side, tall, gorgeously dressed, paying her "much attention."

On the eve of his coronation, Edward VI was obliged to undertake the traditional royal progress from the Tower to Westminster Abbey. That day-long cavalcade is depicted in full in this panorama, which shows the frail, consumptive boy-king and his retinue emerging from the Middle Tower (left) and wending their way through the crowd-lined streets of the city. As the procession advances along Fleet Street (center), through Temple Bar, and out onto the Strand (right), thousands of ordinary citizens gather at bunting-draped windows to catch a glimpse of their new ruler and his court.

She was greeted by the Lord Chancellor, the Marquess of Winchester, and Sir John Brydges, the Lieutenant of the Tower. Winchester knelt down before Lady Jane in order to present her with the keys of the fortress; but her father-in-law, the Duke of Northumberland, stepped forward to receive the keys and handed them to her himself. She then walked on into the inner ward, past lines of Yeomen of the Guard with their gilded axes raised over her shoulders, and entered the royal apartments. She was never to leave the Tower again.

Lady Jane Grey's reign of nine days was a miserable one. She did not fully realize how much her detested father-in-law's political manipulations had angered the people, how strongly they felt that her ill-used cousin Mary was their rightful queen. But she understood only too well that if the Duke of Northumberland succeeded in consolidating his power, she might well be murdered so that he could rule England through his son. If he did not succeed, she would be tried for high treason. In her anxiety her hair began to fall out and her skin to peel.

The defeat of Northumberland's faction by Mary's supporters and the proclamation made at the gates of the Tower — by the Duke of Suffolk, Lady Jane's own father — that Mary was the rightful Queen of England, came as a profound relief to the would-be queen. When Suffolk told Lady Jane what had happened and that she must put off her royal robes and be content with a private life, she replied: "I much more willingly put them off than I put them on. Out of obedience to you, and my mother, I have grievously sinned. Now I willingly relinquish the crown." Then she

asked him if she could go home. Her father did not answer her. He had already made up his mind to save his own neck by leaving her in the Tower to assure Queen Mary of his loyalty. Jane's father-in-law, Northumberland, tried to save himself in the same way, but he was arrested and with his eldest son, the Earl of Warwick — who burst into tears at the sight of the fortress — was escorted to the Tower.

Northumberland was incarcerated in the Beauchamp Tower with Warwick, Lord Guildford Dudley, and his three other sons. Lady Jane, with three female attendants and a page, was transferred from the White Tower to the Gentleman Gaoler's Lodgings on Tower Green. She was allowed writing materials and some books, including her two most valued possessions, her Greek Testament and her prayer book. Strenuous efforts were made to convert Lady Jane to Roman Catholicism while she was in the Gentleman Gaoler's care. But she resisted all blandishments, confidently asserting her unshakable faith in the Protestant religion.

While awaiting execution, Northumberland reaffirmed his belief in the Catholic Church in which he had been brought up and which he had renounced, as he himself confessed, for the sake of ambition. His daughter-in-law, seeing him go to mass in St. Peter ad Vincula, murmured fervently, "I pray God that I, nor no friend of mine, die so."

Northumberland did not die as confidently as Lady Jane was to die. On the scaffold he proclaimed the genuineness of his conversion in a loud voice and enumerated the miseries caused by Protestantism. When the executioner came forward, Northumberland readily gave the man his forgiveness, asking him to do

his part without fear, but when his eyes were bandaged and he began to pray, he nervously mixed up the Lord's Prayer with the Hail Mary. Then the bandage slipped and had to be retied, and Northumberland suddenly displayed his fear. "Surely, he figured to himself the terrible dreadfulness of death," recorded an onlooker. "He smote his hands together as who would say, 'This must be!' — and cast himself on the block."

After Northumberland's body had been taken away to the Chapel of St. Peter ad Vincula, the guards who had been holding back the crowds — ten thousand spectators had gathered on Tower Hill — allowed the people to rush forward with their bits of rags to dip into the blood.

To Lady Jane, Northumberland's execution appeared just reward for his wanton denial of the truths of the Protestant faith, and she did not seem to have regretted her father-in-law's death. In the week that followed she appeared quite content. She was not treated badly, and she was even allowed ninety-three shillings a week, which proved ample for her modest tastes. Occasionally she had dinner with Partridge, the Gentleman Gaoler, and his wife, and was given the place of honor at the head of the table, talking volubly, as was her wont. After her meals, she was allowed by the easygoing lieutenant, Sir John Brydges, whom she described as a "true friend," to walk in his garden. And once or twice she wandered, followed by guards, of course, as far as Tower Hill. She was much more cheerful than she had been as queen, for she had heard that, although she and her husband were to be tried and condemned to death, they would both be pardoned and finally released. Indeed, it is likely that they would have been spared but for the outbreak of an armed rebellion as a result of Queen Mary's unpopular decision to marry Prince Philip, son of Emperor Charles V and soon to be King Philip II of Spain.

The rebellion against the Spanish matrimonial alliance was led by Sir Thomas Wyatt. Son of the poet accused of adultery with Anne Boleyn and godson of the Duke of Norfolk, Wyatt had been one of the closest friends of Norfolk's recently executed son, the Earl of Surrey. Wyatt had accompanied Surrey on wild escapades in London where the two had amused themselves by breaking the windows of houses and churches. Wyatt was in his early thirties when he heard of the proposed royal marriage; and although he seems to have taken little interest in politics until then, he roundly condemned the match as an outrage on the nation's honor and offered to lead an insurgent force on London.

He set out from Kent at the head of four thousand men, encamped at Blackheath south of the river, and on February 3, 1554, entered Southwark. From this position Wyatt demanded the custody of the Tower and of the queen's person and declared his intention of restoring Lady Jane to the throne. When these demands were rejected, he bombarded the Tower from across the river. But his few small cannon were no match for the heavy pieces arrayed on the roof of the White Tower and along Tower Wharf.

Obliged to evacuate Southwark and next failing in a wild attempt to capture the queen at St. James's Palace on the western outskirts of London, Wyatt was captured by the government's forces at Temple Bar and immediately committed to the Tower. He was

*Doomed by her father's ambition and her own
sense of duty, Lady Jane Grey (right) stoically
awaited her turn on Tower Green. From her
vantage in the Gentleman Gaoler's Lodgings (far
right), Lady Jane could see both the path her
tearful husband took to Tower Hill and the
spot — now chained off and marked with a plaque —
where she was to meet her own tearless end.*

executed at Tower Hill on April 11, his body being
subjected to all the grotesque indignities demanded in
cases of treason.

Two days after Wyatt had been brought into the
Tower at the Traitor's Gate — where Sir John Brydges
angrily upbraided him — Lady Jane and her husband
were told that they, too, must now prepare themselves
for death. Lady Jane would be spared, however, if she
became a Roman Catholic. In the hope of being able
to save her, her cousin the queen sent her own confessor, Feckenham, to the Tower.

After his first interview with Lady Jane, Feckenham
was so encouraged that he hurried back to the queen
to ask for a postponement of the date fixed for her
execution. He was confident that, given time, he could
convert her. But the determined and self-possessed
young woman was merely being courteous. When she
was told that the queen had agreed to reprieve her if
she became a Catholic, Lady Jane replied to Feckenham: "Alas! Sir, it was not my desire to prolong my
days. As for death, I utterly despise it, and, Her
Majesty's pleasure being such, I willingly undergo it."
And when Feckenham proposed a public debate, she
rebuked him: "This disputation may be fit for the
living, but not for the dying. Leave me to make my
peace with God."

She was persuaded to change her mind, however, and
the dispute took place in the Chapel of St. Peter ad
Vincula. The outcome was predictable: Lady Jane gave
no ground, and Feckenham had to admit that he had
failed, that he and she would never meet in heaven.
That was true enough, Jane replied, for she would be
there and he would not, unless God sent him His Holy

Spirit and opened the eyes of his heart.

Lady Jane's seventeen-year-old husband, meanwhile,
was displaying no such brave resignation and firm con-
fidence in salvation. He was often in tears and ob-
viously very much afraid. He sought and was granted
permission to say good-by to his wife. But she thought
it best for them not to meet, advising him to "omit
these moments of grief," for they would "shortly behold each other in a better place." She did, however,
agree to stand in the window of her room in the Gentleman Gaoler's Lodgings and to see Lord Guildford
Dudley leave for the scaffold on Tower Hill.

She kept her promise and saw her husband briefly
as he walked across the Green beside the scaffold that
had been erected there for her own execution. He
was crying still, and he went on crying all the way to
Tower Hill. He could not bring himself to make a
speech, but made a "very small declaration" before
falling to his knees with his hands clasped together and
calling out, "Pray for me, pray for me, pray for me."

Guildford Dudley's widow was still standing in the
window of the lodgings when his body was brought
back into the Tower in a handcart. As she caught
sight of it, she was suddenly overcome with pity for
him. "Oh! Guildford! Guildford!" she said, but she
did not weep even then. She had just been examined
"by a body of matrons" to ensure that she was not
pregnant, and she was ready to go to her own death as
soon as the procession had formed up.

She came down the stairs, wearing the black dress
that she had worn at her trial, reading her prayer book,
resting her free hand on the kindly lieutenant's arm.
On the scaffold, composed and clear-voiced, she made

the speech that she had prepared. Feckenham, the Catholic confessor, was by her side. He had asked to be with her at the end, and she, having grown fond of him in their past few days of earnest controversy, had allowed him to come. She turned to him and asked him if she should recite Psalm 51. Overcome with emotion, he could not reply at first, but when he agreed that she should, she knelt down immediately and repeated it, verse by verse. When she had finished, noticing Feckenham's distress, she kissed him and took hold of his hand.

Then she said good-by to the lieutenant and gave him her prayer book, asking him to keep it in memory of her. She gave her handkerchief and gloves to her weeping nurse.

The masked executioner knelt for her forgiveness, and having been granted it, stood up and turned aside, indicating to her that she should now approach the block. For a moment she did not move. The executioner urged her, "Stand upon the straw, Madam."

She approached the block then, but suddenly she turned again and said, "You will not take it off before I lay me down."

"No, Madam."

She tied her handkerchief around her eyes, and sank to her knees. She put out her hands to feel the block, but she was too far away from it and her fingers fluttered in the air. "Where is it?" she called out.

As though they were paralyzed by her pathetic plight, no one on the scaffold came forward to help her. "What shall I do?" she pleaded, "What shall I do?" For the first time it seemed that she might break down. Still no one on the scaffold could bring himself to move. In the end it was one of the spectators standing beyond the rail who came forward to guide her. She placed her bared neck into the curve and cried out in a loud voice: "Lord into Thy hands I commend my spirit!"

Her body was taken away and buried with that of her husband in the Chapel of St. Peter ad Vincula — not far from the tomb of her father-in-law, Northumberland, who lay beside his victim, the Duke of Somerset. It was July 1554, one year after Lady Jane's rash and ambitious relatives had tried to thrust her on the throne of England.

Soon after Lady Jane's death, her cousin Princess Elizabeth, also compromised by Wyatt's rebellion, was brought a prisoner to the Tower.

Elizabeth, the Protestant daughter of Henry VIII by the ill-fated Anne Boleyn, had been raised by a succession of guardians, but she had been given a complete and enlightened education as befitted a woman of the Renaissance. In these years Elizabeth was also gaining valuable knowledge of the arts of political intrigue and government. She had seen her younger half brother, Edward, feebly rule for six years and then had witnessed the folly of Lady Jane Grey's brief reign. At the accession to the throne in 1553 of her older half sister, Mary, she was twenty years old. Although next in line to the throne, Elizabeth became Mary's prisoner.

It was on a Sunday that Elizabeth was brought to the Tower, and it was raining. She was as desolate as she had ever been in her life, recalling, no doubt, with deep foreboding that her mother had died within these very same gray walls.

As Elizabeth's barge approached Traitor's Gate, she begged to be landed anywhere but there. When her request was coldly refused, her misery turned into angry indignation. A lord attending her offered her his cloak to protect her from the rain, but she scornfully rejected his offer, pushing his cloak away from her "with a good dash." And as soon as she stepped ashore on the landing steps she exclaimed crossly, "Here landeth as true a subject, being prisoner, as ever landed at these stairs," adding for the benefit of the warders lined up to receive her on the other side of Traitor's Gate, "Oh Lord! I never thought to have come in here as a prisoner; and I pray you all, bear me witness that I come in as no traitor but as true a woman to the Queen's Majesty as any as is now living." Then she sat down on a stone, and refused to move. The lieutenant came forward and urged her to rise, if only to get out of the rain. "Better," she said, "to sit here than in a worse place, for God knoweth where you will bring me."

For two months Elizabeth was kept in the Tower, while the government vainly tried to find evidence upon which to convict her of complicity in the Wyatt rebellion. Stephen Gardiner, Bishop of Winchester and Lord Chancellor, strongly urged that she be sent to the block as Lady Jane Grey had been.

While waiting for her fate to be decided, the princess was at first treated well by the kindhearted Sir John Brydges, but when Sir John Gage, the constable, discovered how many indulgences were being granted her by the lieutenant, he immediately put a stop to them. Gage, a zealous Catholic, expressly forbade her servants to bring her provisions, requiring instead that

they hand them over at the gates where the "common rascal soldiers" ate what they fancied before giving the rest to the prisoners. Gage also forbade her to leave her lodgings for the first month of her imprisonment. When her health began to suffer and she had to be allowed out to walk in the garden, he ordered that she was always to be accompanied by a guard. Even a girl of four who came up to her with a present of a bunch of flowers was closely questioned in the belief that she was the bearer of secret messages.

Although all those implicated in Wyatt's rebellion were carefully questioned, and one of the principal conspirators who had been a member of the princess's household was "marvellously tossed and examined," no evidence against Elizabeth could be unearthed. After spending two months in the Tower, she was released to an easier confinement at the royal manor of Woodstock in Oxfordshire.

Those whose loyalty to Queen Mary was more easily disproved were not so fortunate. Thomas Cranmer, Archbishop of Canterbury, who had unwillingly been dragged into the Duke of Northumberland's plot to place Lady Jane Grey upon the throne, was brought to the Tower with two other bishops, Hugh Latimer, Bishop of Worcester, and Nicholas Ridley, Bishop of London. By then the Tower was so crowded with other suspected traitors that at first they all had to sleep together in one room, where they were even denied the comfort of a fire. In complaining to the warders, Latimer, a very old man, shortly to be burned at the stake like the other two bishops, observed with gentle irony: "I suppose you expect me to be burned, but unless you let me have some fire, I am likely to deceive your expectations, for I shall most probably die of the cold."

The sudden death of Queen Mary on November 17, 1558, brought to an end the persecution of her Protestant subjects, a persecution for which she earned the name Bloody Mary. But in the reign of Mary's half sister, Elizabeth, who succeeded her, the privations of Roman Catholics held in the Tower for their conscience's sake were even more severe. Of these, none suffered as pitifully as John Gerard, a Jesuit priest sent as a missionary to his home country by the English College at Rome, who was savagely tortured in the Tower's dungeons.

Although Gerard's hands, black and swollen, were paralyzed as a result of the tortures to which he had been subjected, the priest happily managed to effect his escape. He did so by means of a rope, the method most commonly employed by those few prisoners who had succeeded in escaping from the Tower in the previous five centuries of its existence.

The first to get away by using a rope was Bishop Rannulf Flambard, who had been imprisoned in the Tower by Henry I, the son of William the Conqueror. Flambard had undoubtedly been the most detested man in the kingdom, having encouraged his late master, William Rufus, in his every iniquity. Yet Flambard's imprisonment in the Tower had been scarcely worse than an inconvenience. He had been permitted to keep a sumptuous table for himself and his servants and to enjoy most of the pleasures to which he had been devoted while free. He had managed to escape while his keepers were sitting drunkenly at his table after a banquet that he had provided for them.

Making use of a rope that had been smuggled into the Tower inside a cask of wine, Flambard had clambered down from the window of his room. Although it was his lissome figure and extraordinary good looks that had first gained him notice at William the Conqueror's court, by the time of his imprisonment he had become a fat and clumsy man, and he had found the climb an arduous one, particularly as he had insisted on carrying his pastoral staff in one hand. The rope had proved too short, and he had fallen the last few feet to the ground. But there had been a fast horse awaiting him, and he had been able to make good his escape to France.

In the century after Flambard's escape, Griffin, eldest son of Llewellyn, Prince of Wales, had also attempted to escape from the Tower by using a rope. Eluding the vigilance of his jailers, he had tied the rope to one of the battlements of the turret in which he was confined and climbed out into the darkness. Unfortunately, the rope broke, and Griffin's corpse was found the next morning at the foot of the turret, his head crushed down beneath his shoulders.

Father Gerard was both more ingenious than Flambard and more fortunate than Griffin. He broke out of the Salt Tower in a remarkable manner, by persuading his jailer to let him visit John Arden, a fellow Roman Catholic. Arden was incarcerated in the Cradle Tower, a building only 150 feet to the south of the Salt Tower but on the other side of the outer ward, overlooking the moat. One day Gerard managed to carry to the Cradle Tower, concealed in the skirts of his cassock, a length of strong thin cord that he had obtained from friends in London by sending them a message written in an invisible ink made from orange juice. At an appointed hour one night, a lead weight attached to the end of his cord was hurled across the moat, and over Tower Wharf beyond it, to a man waiting in a boat on the river. This man tied a rope to the cord and Arden then pulled up the end of the rope to the window of his cell. Squeezing through the window between the bars and the stone wall, Gerard — despite his paralyzed hands — managed to slide down the rope into the boat.

Elizabeth's great rival was her Catholic cousin Mary Queen of Scots. Until her execution in the great hall of Fotheringay Castle in 1587, Mary's adherents were almost as frequently to be found as prisoners in the Tower as were Jesuits. The first of Mary's supporters to suffer there was Thomas Howard, fourth Duke of Norfolk — son of the Earl of Surrey who had been beheaded in the Tower in 1547, and grandson of the third duke who had been saved from a similar fate himself by the death of Henry VIII. As a Roman Catholic, the third duke had remained in the Tower throughout the reign of Edward VI but had been released on Queen Mary's accession and had commanded her forces against the rebel, Sir Thomas Wyatt. Failing to distinguish himself in that action, the duke had retired after the rebellion to his house in Norfolk, where he died in 1554.

His grandson, who became the fourth Duke of Norfolk at the age of eighteen, was too young to take any important part in the events of Queen Mary's reign. But on the death of his third wife, when he was only thirty-two and already the richest man in England, Norfolk offered himself in marriage to Mary Queen of

Scots. The decision brought him into immediate conflict with the young Queen Elizabeth, and in October 1569 he found himself a prisoner in the Tower. Although released on that occasion, Norfolk was condemned to death in 1572 for treason after he was implicated in a plot to bring about a Spanish invasion of England. He died composedly on Tower Hill, surrounded by a "vast crowd of gazing spectators," refusing the offer of a handkerchief with which to bandage his eyes.

Some time later Francis Throckmorton, who had also discussed the possibility of gaining the throne of England for Mary Queen of Scots through an invasion by Spanish troops, was arrested, imprisoned, tortured, and executed. A subsequent supporter of Mary's, Henry Percy, eighth Earl of Northumberland, contrived to evade the executioner. Determined that Queen Elizabeth should not appropriate his property, as she would have the right to do if he had been found guilty and condemned for high treason, Northumberland was heard one day to murmur, "The bitch at least shall not have my estate." Shortly afterward he was found in his cell with the door locked on the inside and a pistol on the floor by his bed. He had evidently shot himself through the heart.

Undeterred by the failure of earlier conspirators, John Ballard, a Jesuit priest, and Anthony Babington, the rich young son of an ancient Roman Catholic family of Derbyshire, conceived a daring plan, in 1586, for a general uprising of Catholics, the murder of Queen Elizabeth, and the accession of Mary to the English throne. The plot was soon discovered, however, and Ballard, Babington, and twelve wild young conspira-

tors associated with them were all arrested, brought to the Tower, and condemned to traitors' deaths. No part of the hideous sentence was commuted. Ballard was hanged first and brought down alive from the gallows to be dismembered and disembowelled. "Babington looked on with an undaunted countenance," an observer recorded, "steadily gazing on that variety of tortures which he himself in a moment [was] to pass through. . . . When the executioner began his tremendous work on Babington, the spirit of this haughty and heroic man cried out amidst the agony, *'Parce mihi, Domine Jesu!'* There were two days of executions."

When she heard reports of the hideous brutalities of the first day, Queen Elizabeth ordered that the rest of the conspirators should be hanged until they were dead. For she was not a cruel woman and had a real horror of bloodshed. But she had no hesitation in punishing with the greatest severity anyone found guilty of an attempt on her life — and for this crime two country gentlemen were imprisoned in the Tower, hanged, disembowelled, and quartered in 1583. Otherwise the only offenses that appeared to excite Elizabeth's fears and anger were those connected with what were known as "love matters." Even then, prisoners confined in the Tower for these transgressions were never harshly treated, as was shown by the imprisonment of Lady Catherine Grey.

Lady Catherine, Lady Jane's sister, the next person in the succession to the throne under the will of Henry VIII, had enraged Elizabeth by marrying the Earl of Hertford without her consent. She had then compounded this folly by becoming pregnant, thus making declaration to the world that she was more

worthy of the throne than the barren "virgin queen." Both the earl and his countess were consigned to the Tower for their reckless behavior, but their confinement was not particularly irksome. Lady Hertford was allowed to furnish her apartments with costly curtains, tapestries, and Turkish carpets, a fine bed with a feather mattress, and a chair upholstered in cloth of gold and crimson velvet. She was also permitted what food she liked, the company of her pet dogs and monkeys, and visits from her husband. It was not until — to the disgust and outrage of the queen — a second baby was born to Lady Hertford that her pleasures were denied her by the abrupt dismissal of the obliging lieutenant, Sir Edward Warner.

The Countess of Hertford was not the only one of the queen's ladies-in-waiting to suffer in the Tower for an indiscreet love affair. The Countess of Lennox was imprisoned there three times for "love matters." And it was his intrigue with Bess Throckmorton — whom he later secretly married — that led to Sir Walter Ralegh's first imprisonment in the Tower in 1592. Although it was to be four years before Ralegh was readmitted to the queen's presence, this was a relatively brief imprisonment. When he was consigned to the Tower a second time, in 1603, after Elizabeth's death, he was not to leave it for thirteen years.

For this second imprisonment, Ralegh's alleged offense was treason. But after he had brilliantly disposed of the flimsy charges at his trial, no one doubted that his real offense was having aroused the animosity and jealousy of King James I, son of Mary Queen of Scots, who succeeded to the English throne at the death of Queen Elizabeth. (See chart, page 168.) Despite the

George Turberville, poet and self-appointed arbiter of sixteenth-century court etiquette, published The Noble Arte of Venerie or Hunting in 1575. Among the topics covered in that illustrated protocol was "the place where and howe an assembly should be made" for a royal outing such as the elaborate picnic seen at right.

success of his defense, Ralegh was condemned to death, and not until he was actually upon the scaffold was the sentence commuted to one of life imprisonment. He was the most respected and adulated prisoner the Tower had ever held. Crowds flocked to the walls in the hope of catching sight of him on the wall between the Bloody Tower and the Lieutenant's Lodgings as he took the daily walk that he was allowed. When he appeared, the crowd waved and cheered, and he would turn to face them, bowing gravely.

The more distinguished of Ralegh's admirers called upon the lieutenant to ask permission to visit the great man. Ambassadors and courtiers came, noblemen and rich merchants from the city; the king's Danish queen came and so did his gifted, intelligent son Henry, Prince of Wales. "Only my father," Henry said, revealing his contempt for the king, "only my father would keep such a bird in a cage."

James tried to put a stop to the adulation of Ralegh and the indulgence shown to him by dismissing the sympathetic lieutenant, Sir George Harvey, and appointing the perverse and embittered Sir William Waad in his place. Waad, who had played a leading part in getting Ralegh convicted at his trial, now did his best to make his confinement less comfortable. He harassed Ralegh with petty restrictions: refused him the freedom of the lieutenant's garden where he had formerly tended the flowers, declined permission for Lady Ralegh's coach to enter the Tower gate, dismissed the black servants whom Ralegh had brought back from Guiana and whom he had been allowed to take with him into the Bloody Tower. But so influential were Ralegh's friends that even Waad could not make his

prisoner's life as unpleasant as he would have liked.

Ralegh continued to receive visits from the Prince of Wales and was able to talk to him at length about history, astronomy, and seamanship. He occupied his time by making models of ships, by writing what he intended to be a history of the whole world "beginning with the creation," and by conducting scientific experiments in a little hen house by the garden wall which he had converted into a laboratory. Occasionally his wife was allowed to visit him. In the days of Sir George Harvey's lieutenancy, Lady Ralegh had actually lived in the Bloody Tower with her husband, and their second son Carew was born there. But Waad had ejected her and she had moved into a house on Tower Hill.

Soon afterward, Ralegh's doctor obtained permission for him to leave the Bloody Tower. Sir Walter was afflicted with rheumatism and a growing palsy that the doctor attributed to a recent close confinement in a damp dungeon of the Bloody Tower as a punishment for some offense against the lieutenant's rules. The patient's left arm and hand were affected, and it was feared that unless he were moved his power of speech would be altogether lost. So a small room was built for him adjoining his laboratory by the garden wall, and there, as the long months passed, he slowly regained his strength. When he was well again, he was moved to lodgings in the Brick Tower overlooking the moat on the fortress's northern side.

In 1610, Ralegh sought permission to guide an expedition of adventurers to the region of the Orinoco, a river in the north of South America. He believed they might find there rich deposits of gold. "If I bring them not to a mountain covered with gold and silver ore,"

THE
HISTORIE OF
THE WORLD.

IN FIVE BOOKES.

1 ENtreating of the Beginning and first Ages of the same, from the Creation unto Abraham.

2 Of the Times from the Birth of Abraham, to the destruction of the Temple of Salomon.

3 From the destruction of Jerusalem, to the time of Philip of Macedon.

4 From the Reigne of Philip of Macedon, to the establishing of that Kingdome, in the Race of Antigonus.

5 From the settled rule of Alexanders Successors in the East, untill the Romans (prevailing over all) made Conquest of Asia and Macedon.

By Sir WALTER RALEGH, Knight.

VERA EFFIGIES CLARISSIMI VIRI GUALTHERI RALEGH EQV AUR. etc. IN DOM.

Sim: Pass: sculp: Comp: Holland exc:

AMORE ET VIRTVTE

The true and lively portraiture of the honourable and learned Knight Sr. Walter Ralegh.

The most revered prisoner the Tower ever held was Sir Walter Ralegh, the English navigator, courtier, poet, and historian who devoted his second confinement in the Bloody Tower to drafting a mammoth, five-volume history of the world. The title page of Ralegh's first volume, which was published while its author was still imprisoned, indicates the manner in which the ill-fated nobleman preferred to spell his name.

he wrote, "let the commander have commission to cut off my head there."

After a long delay, King James was prevailed upon to grant permission for the voyage, and Ralegh was released from the Tower. Having ventured all he had on the enterprise, Sir Walter set sail from Plymouth in June 1617. From the very beginning the undertaking seemed doomed to failure: the weather was foul, ships were disabled, water ran short, the crews were stricken with scurvy and fever, and when they landed, the Spaniards blocked their path to the mine. Dejected by his failure, Ralegh returned to England and, attempting to escape to France from Plymouth, was arrested and brought back to the Tower. There he was informed that he was to be executed in accordance with the sentence for treason passed upon him fifteen years earlier.

Sir Walter Ralegh faced death without a tremor. On the scaffold he asked the headsman if he might feel the axe to make sure that it was sharp enough. The headsman hesitated until Ralegh urged him with easy courtesy, "I pray thee let me feel it." He touched the edge with his fingers and, smiling, turned to the sheriff. "This is a sharp medicine," he said, "but it is a physician for all diseases."

To the executioner he said: "When I stretch forth my hands despatch me." He declined to be blindfolded, remarking that he was not likely to fear the shadow of the axe since he did not fear the axe itself. When he lay down with his head on the block, one of the king's chaplains asked him if he did not think he ought to be lying with his head facing east, "for our Lord's rising."

"If the heart be right," Ralegh replied, "it is no matter which way the head lieth."

The headsman was trembling so much that he could not bring himself to strike the blow when the signal was given. After a pause, Ralegh stretched out his hands once more, but again the headsman did not move. As though paralyzed by his convulsive trembling, he remained with the axe at his side while the crowd watched and waited.

"What dost thou fear?" Ralegh called out in his strong clear voice. "Strike, man, strike!"

The headsman struck then, but it was a fumbling blow, and the axe had to be raised again. Ralegh's body "never shrank nor moved." The second blow severed the head, and the headsman held it up by the hair in silence, unwilling or unable to repeat the customary phrases. In the momentary quiet, a man in the crowd called out instead: "We have not another such head to be cut off!"

So died the last of the Elizabethans.

V

IN DUNGEONS DIRE

Meeting early in 1604 in an upper room of a small house beyond Clement's Inn, five men knelt to receive the sacrament. The officiating priest was the Jesuit John Gerard, who had bravely continued his missionary activities in the city after his remarkable escape from the Tower a few years earlier. The five communicants had just taken a solemn oath to keep secret all that had been discussed in the house that day; they had sworn never to divulge the particulars of a daring plan they had devised to seize the government and to kill King James I, Elizabeth's Protestant successor. This plan was to be known to history as the Gunpowder Plot.

The plot was one of astonishing audacity. It involved the renting of a tenement adjoining the parliament house, the construction of a mine in its cellar to run beneath the neighboring buildings, the storing in this mine of vast quantities of gunpowder, and — when James was speaking in the House of Lords — the ignition of a fuse that would destroy the king, Lords, and Commons in one gigantic explosion and thus rock the state to its very foundations.

One of the conspirators was a young Yorkshire-born convert to Roman Catholicism who had served with distinction as a soldier of fortune in the Spanish army. His name was Guy — or, as he preferred, Guido — Fawkes. Calling himself Johnson, he was to take possession of the house next door to parliament and later, dressed as a porter, to keep watch at its door while the other conspirators dug their mine. In December the digging began and for more than a fortnight, while Fawkes stood sentinel, his companions tunneled and burrowed their way beneath the parliament house. At the beginning of the following year, however, an adjoining cellar that ran immediately below the House of Lords fell vacant, and so the conspirators rented this in the name of one of their number, Thomas Percy, a gentleman pensioner whom the authorities had little reason to suspect of any evil design. This cellar was filled with barrels of gunpowder and iron bars concealed beneath a pile of lumber. Fawkes was to fire the charge with a slow match on the day that Parliament was due to meet, November 5, 1605.

All might well have gone as planned had not some of the conspirators wished to warn their Catholic friends in the Lords not to attend Parliament that day. One of the peers, warned in an ambiguous, unsigned letter, was Lord Monteagle, and he immediately took his letter to Lord Salisbury, the king's principal secretary of state. The cellar was searched, the gunpowder discovered, and Fawkes arrested with slow matches and touchwood in his possession.

At one o'clock in the morning Fawkes was brought to face the council in the king's bedchamber at Whitehall Palace. He appeared completely unmoved by his predicament and insisted that his name was Johnson, although he did not deny that his intention had been to blow up Parliament. His only regret, he said, was that he had not succeeded in doing so, that he had failed to blow the Scottish king and his Scottish followers back to Scotland where they belonged. He refused, however, to answer any questions about his fellow conspirators. He was therefore taken away to be submitted to more rigorous questioning in the torture chamber in the basement of the White Tower.

It was the pride of the English common law that it did not recognize torture as legal. It had always favored an accusatorial system, in which the accuser had to prove guilt, rather than an inquisitorial system, in which the accused had to prove innocence; and it had therefore theoretically discountenanced the violent methods by which confessions were obtained on the Continent. Nevertheless, torture had in fact often been used in criminal trials in England after a warrant had been obtained from the council and was, indeed, sometimes used without a warrant. Also prisoners had been tortured by license of the king at least as early as the reign of Henry II (1154–89) when a royal warrant was issued to the mayor and sheriffs of London to torture the Knights Templar in order to elicit from them confessions of homosexuality and other malpractices for which they were later condemned.

The rack at the Tower was in common use by the reign of Henry VI (1422–61). It was introduced, it is believed, by the Duke of Exeter, who was appointed Constable of the Tower for life in 1420, and it was therefore known as the Duke of Exeter's Daughter. In the sixteenth century the Scavenger's Daughter, introduced by Sir Leonard Skevington, Lieutenant of the Tower in the reign of Henry VIII, was also in frequent and authorized use. This was a device that crushed the body until the blood spurted out of the nostrils and the tips of the fingers instead of, like the rack, stretching it "until the bones and joints were almost plucked asunder." The use of both the Scavenger's Daughter and the rack became more and more common under the Tudors, and by the latter part of the reign of Elizabeth I, the rack, it was said, "seldom stood idle in the Tower."

The rack was a rectangular frame of wood with

Determined to rid England of its Scottish king, a fanatical band of regicides including "Guido" Fawkes (left) hatched a plot to level Parliament and James I with a single blast of gunpowder. Exposed, incarcerated, and later interrogated in the council chamber (below), Fawkes vehemently denied his involvement in the conspiracy — and it was not until James ordered "the gentler tortours" applied that Fawkes confessed his guilt.

short supports that kept it raised slightly from the ground. The legs of a prisoner were fastened to a fixed bar at the bottom end, and the wrists to a movable bar above his head. By pulling on a lever attached to the movable bar the limbs were slowly stretched, with increasing agony to the sufferer, until they were eventually dislocated. Some victims died on the rack; others were permanently crippled by its tortures; most confessed to all manner of crimes, real or imagined, at the first exquisite pangs of pain — or even at the very sight of the dreaded instrument.

The Jesuit martyr Edmund Campion was brought to the Tower in 1581 through jeering crowds, with his elbows tied behind him, his hands tied in front, his feet strapped under the horse's belly, and with a notice in his hat announcing his identity as "Campion, the seditious Jesuit." He was racked so severely that he never recovered. The next day when his jailer asked him how he felt Campion replied, "not ill, because not at all." Three weeks later he could not lift up his hand high enough to take the oath.

Anne Askew, a Protestant who held various beliefs condemned as heretical, was racked in the Tower in the reign of Henry VIII. She was tortured so savagely that she was never afterward able to walk; she had to be carried strapped to a chair to be burned at the stake in Smithfield. In the hope that they could extract from her the names of her fellow sectarians, Thomas Wriothesley, the Lord Chancellor, and Sir Richard Rich, his future successor, turned the lever with their own hands, "straining it with all their force," as they asked their persistent questions. Twice she fainted, yet she would tell them nothing nor change her opinions. When, nearly dead, she was removed from the rack at the insistence of the lieutenant, she lay for two hours on the bare floor where she nevertheless continued to summon the energy to refute the Lord Chancellor's arguments.

Father John Gerard, who was tortured in the Tower in 1597 and succeeded in escaping from it though his hands had been almost paralyzed, was racked repeatedly. He described how he was led down into the torture chamber through subterranean passages lighted by candles. "It was a place of immense extent," he wrote, "and in it were arranged divers sorts of racks, and other instruments of torture. Some of these they displayed before me, and told me that I should have to taste them. They then led me to a great upright beam or pillar of wood, which was one of the supports of this vast crypt." He was strung up for an hour to this beam, suspended by his hands in iron gauntlets; he was a heavy man and the agony made him faint several times. The lieutenant, William Waad — "that beast Waad" in Ralegh's description — demanded a confession; and when Gerard refused to recant his faith, Waad shouted at him, "Hang you there till you rot." The priest fainted again and was taken down. The next day Waad conducted him to the rack master to whom he said: "I deliver this man into your hands. You are to rack him twice a day until such time as he chooses to confess." But at the time of his escape the indomitable Gerard had confessed nothing.

Although the rack was the most commonly used instrument of torture in the sixteenth century, there were several others apart from it and the Scavenger's Daughter. Some are now merely names whose method of inflicting pain can only be guessed at. There were the boot, the thumbscrew, the caschie-laws, the lang-irnis, the narrow-bore, the iron collar, the pynebankis, the bilboes (which compressed the ankles), the pilli-winks (which squeezed the fingers), and the brakes (a fearful device for breaking the prisoner's teeth, which was used in the Tower to elicit confessions from those accused of misconduct with Catherine Howard). Prisoners were also tortured by subjecting them to the *tormento de toca,* the maddening pouring of water, drop by drop, on a particular part of the body, usually the forehead; by the pouring of water into a gauze bag in the throat, which slowly forced the gauze down the stomach; and by burning the soles of the feet at a fire.

A common torture inflicted upon prisoners who refused to plead guilty was the *peine forte et dure,* or pressing to death. The object of submitting to this was that the estate of a man who died under torture could be willed to his chosen heirs, whereas if he were tried and found guilty it would pass to the crown. The *peine forte et dure* was recognized by the common law — although not specifically as a torture — and was not finally abolished until the reign of George III, a victim suffering under its agonies as late as 1726.

The terrible words containing the threat of *peine forte et dure* were uttered according to a formula little altered since the early fifteenth century, when pressing to death took the place of starving to death because it was quicker and considered more humane. Three times the prisoner was warned of the consequences of his obstinacy. If he continued obstinate, sentence was passed that he "shall be remanded to the place from whence he came, and put in some low dark room; he

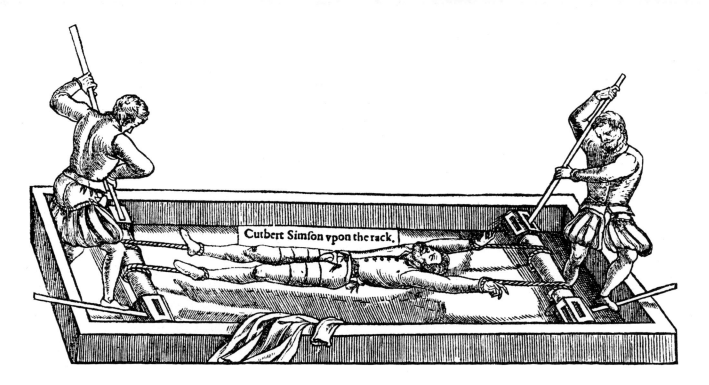

Cutbert Simſon vpon the rack.

shall lie without any litter or anything under him, and that one arm shall be drawn to one quarter of the room with a cord, and the other to another, and that his feet shall be used in the same manner, and that as many weights shall be laid on him as he can bear and more. That he shall have three morsels of barley bread a day, and that he shall have the water next the prison, so that it be not current, and that he shall not eat the same day upon which he drinks, nor drink the same day upon which he eats; and he shall so continue till he die."

As well as the press room in which the *peine forte et dure* was carried out, most prisons had at least one cell in which a victim could be incarcerated in the most painful discomfort. In the Tower this cell was known as the Little Ease, a dungeon so small that it was impossible either to stand upright in it or to lie at full length. There, before being racked, Edmund Campion was kept crouching in the dark for four days.

According to one authority, Guy Fawkes was also placed in the Little Ease after his return from his interrogation at Whitehall on the morning of November 5. Certainly, after being further examined by a special commission in the council chamber in the Lieutenant's Lodgings, he was placed on the rack in accordance with the orders of the king, who had written to the commission: "if he will not other wayes confesse, the gentler tortours are to be first usid unto him *et sic per gradus ad ima tenditur* [and so on step by step to the most severe] and so god spede youre goode worke." For half an hour Fawkes endured the torture as the screws were turned and then he gasped out that he would tell all he knew of the plot. His confession was written down, and he signed it with a weak and trembling hand.

It was suggested that after his execution Fawkes's body should be hung in chains outside the parliament house as a dreadful warning to other would-be traitors. This was not done, but a few years after his death a body *was* hung in chains facing the Tower. This was the tarred corpse of Sir Gervase Helwys, Lieutenant of the Tower, who had been implicated in a terrible crime.

Helwys was appointed lieutenant in May 1613, a fortnight after the committal to the Tower of Sir Thomas Overbury, secretary and friend of Robert Carr, Viscount Rochester. Rochester had come from Scotland as page to King James, whose taste for handsome young men was notorious, and he had, through the king's favor, achieved great influence at court. In 1613 he had become the lover of the sultry, sensual, and unbalanced daughter of the Earl of Suffolk, Lady Frances Howard, who had been married at the age of thirteen to the Earl of Essex. Frances Howard was determined to divorce Essex, on the alleged grounds of his impotence, and to marry her lover, Rochester. But standing in her way was Sir Thomas Overbury who, though happy enough that his friend and patron should be the lover of Lady Frances, strongly advised him against marrying so unsuitable and unstable a girl.

To rid herself of Overbury, who knew so much about her past life that he might have been able to prevent her marriage to Rochester, Lady Frances induced her family and her lover to press for his imprisonment at the Tower on the flimsy charge that he had acted "contrary to the orders of his Sovereign Lord

*To rid herself of Sir Thomas Overbury (right),
who opposed her impending remarriage, the willful
and unbalanced Lady Frances Howard had her
detractor committed to the Tower — where she
systematically poisoned him with arsenic-laced
tarts. After three agonizing months, Overbury
succumbed and was buried in the Chapel of
St. Peter ad Vincula (opposite), whose marble floor
is inlaid with the names of other notable prisoners —
among them the Earl of Northumberland — who
died within the walls of the Tower.*

the King" by refusing to accept a diplomatic appointment abroad. Overbury was accordingly arrested and "by warrant consigned to the Lieutenant of the Tower as close prisoner" on April 26, 1613.

The lieutenant at this time was still that William Waad who had aroused the hatred of Ralegh and who had supervised the tortures of Father Gerard and Guy Fawkes. He seems to have been a harsh, uncouth man, but he was evidently not a corruptible one. Lady Frances thought it better that Waad should be induced to retire in favor of the more pliable Sir Gervase Helwys, a protégé of her family who could be persuaded to do what he was told. On receipt of two thousand pounds in compensation for his loss of office, Waad retired and Helwys took his place. The warder in charge of the Bloody Tower was also dismissed, in favor of one Richard Weston, a disreputable character in the employ of Mrs. Anne Turner, known to Lady Frances as a brothel owner, an abortionist, and — more important to her present purpose — a dealer in love philters and other dubious medicaments.

With the help of her unsavory accomplices and undeterred by the half-hearted attempts of Sir Gervase Helwys to prevent a crime that might lead to his downfall, Lady Frances now set about murdering Sir Thomas Overbury by poison. To his cell in the Bloody Tower she sent poisoned tarts and poisoned jellies; she had his wine poisoned with mercury sublimate, his partridges with lapis costitus; she had white and red arsenic mixed with his salt, cantharides with his pepper, and lunar caustic (silver nitrate) with his pork. She plied him with "Great Spiders" and aqua fortis (nitric acid) and powdered diamonds. She gave him —

as her supplier, Mrs. Turner, afterward confessed — enough poison to kill twenty men, but he continued to survive. He relapsed into fever; he vomited; he fainted. A drunken servant, taking some tarts into Overbury's cell, spilled a little syrup over his hands; he licked it off and within a few days most of his hair and several of his fingernails had fallen out. Yet it was not until a corrupt apothecary's assistant administered an enema to him that Overbury — who astonishingly never seems to have suspected what was being done to him — eventually succumbed, three and a half months after his first imprisonment.

A verdict of accidental death was immediately pronounced, and Sir Thomas was buried that same afternoon in the Chapel of St. Peter ad Vincula. It was not until two years later, in 1615, that the truth came out, through the dying confessions of one of Lady Frances's accomplices. Both Rochester and Lady Frances, by then the Earl and Countess of Somerset, were arrested and brought to the Tower. The countess was at first led to the very cell in the Bloody Tower where Sir Thomas had died; but at the sight of it she almost fainted and shrieked: "Put me not in there; his ghost will haunt me!" So her husband was put there in her place; and she was given quarters in the room that Ralegh had used as his laboratory. Although they were eventually pardoned by the king, they were both kept in the Tower for many years, their love for each other gradually turning to hatred. Lady Somerset, insane, died of cancer of the womb eleven years after her release; her husband lived on in obscurity until 1645.

Lady Somerset's accomplices were less fortunate. Mrs. Turner and Richard Weston were hanged at

Tyburn. Sir Gervase Helwys was executed on Tower Hill, and his body was hung in chains in full view of the prison he had once commanded.

The year after Overbury's poisoning, there was another death at the Tower that might equally well be described as murder. This was the death of Lord Grey of Wilton, who was arrested at the same time as Sir Walter Ralegh on suspicion of being involved in a plot to place a more suitable candidate than James I on the throne of England. Grey was imprisoned at the Tower with Lady Arabella Stuart, a cousin of the king. Lady Arabella's unauthorized marriage to a grandson of Lady Catherine Grey, Lady Jane Grey's sister, had aroused King James's fears that she intended to supplant him. On the accusation that he had "had conference" with one of Lady Arabella's maids, Lord Grey was kept in such severe and repressive confinement that he languished and died at the Tower in 1614.

Sir John Eliot, another victim of Stuart animosity, met a similar fate a few years later. Eliot was a leading member of the House of Commons; and his venomous attacks on the court favorite George Villiers, Duke of Buckingham, earned him the implacable hatred of Charles I, son and successor of King James. In 1629 Eliot, with eight other members of the House, was sent to the Tower, where he refused to acknowledge himself in error and was thus kept in conditions of dreadful squalor.

The Tower regulations of 1607, which were still in force, decreed that "when the Bell doth ring at nights for the shutting in of the gates, all the prisoners, with their servants, are to withdraw themselves into their chambers, and not to goe forth that night." But these regulations did not apply to Eliot, who was denied all such privileges as exercise in the hours of daylight, apart from a few steps each day along the platform of a wall outside his cell door. He was allowed only occasional visitors and they were limited to his doctor, his servant, and the eldest of his five sons. Sometimes he was even denied the use of candles; he had either to accept the cold and damp or endure a cell whose stale air was filled with smoke from an unvented fire.

After three years of this treatment Eliot contracted tuberculosis, and he wrote to the king to petition for his freedom: "By reason of the quality of the air, I am fallen into a dangerous disease. I humbly beseech Your Majesty you will command your judge to set me at liberty that, for the recovery of my health, I may take some fresh air." Charles, noting the absence of remorse or even of apology for Eliot's vendetta against his beloved Buckingham, or for what he took to be the man's crimes against the state, refused the request; a second petition received no answer at all. In November 1632 Eliot, aged forty, died at the Tower.

Eliot's son asked permission to remove his father's body for burial in the Cornish churchyard where his family and ancestors lay. The request received a brief reply: "Let Sir John Eliot be buried in that parish wherein he died." Thus Parliament in its worsening quarrel with the king was given its first martyr.

Well aware of the Tower's real and symbolic importance in this quarrel, Charles determined to keep control of it when the differences between him and his enemies threatened to erupt into a civil war between his supporters, the Cavaliers, and the champions of Parliament, later to be known as the Roundheads. The king dismissed the constable, Lord Newport, one of the crown's leading opponents, and he replaced the Puritan lieutenant, Sir William Balfour, with Colonel Thomas Lunsford, a royalist soldier of fortune and a "very desperate" man who could be relied upon to defend it to the death. Colonel Lunsford's outrageously provocative behavior, however, did more to harm the king's cause than to save it. He strode threateningly along Tower Wharf and the ramparts, sword in hand. He strutted about New Palace Yard outside Westminster Hall, making insulting remarks about the king's enemies. And one day, "brandishing his sword, he rushed into the Hall with about a dozen other gentlemen, chasing the citizens about the Hall. He and his friends then made their way through those who were in Palace Yard and King Street till they came to Whitehall."

The House of Commons condemned Lunsford as an outlaw, a heathen, "a ruined and desperate character." In London, he was widely rumored to be a cannibal with a highly developed taste for the flesh of babies. The reiterated cry of the apprentices the Christmas of 1641 was, "No Bishops! No Lords! Down with Butcher Lunsford." Even to devoted Cavaliers, he seemed a dangerous ruffian; and the Lord Mayor of London, Sir Richard Gurney, a faithful royalist, begged the king to remove the colonel from his post at the Tower. At length Charles agreed to do so; but he was careful to replace him with Sir John Byron, a man of royalist sympathies as unmistakable as Lunsford's.

Sir John Byron immediately displayed his spirit and enterprise. He entered the historic fortress with a strong detachment of gunners, disarmed the Trained Bands — London's militiamen — who had occupied the Tower in Lunsford's absence, and prepared to defend it against all comers. After the king fled London on January 10, 1642, following his disastrously unsuccessful attempt to arrest five of his leading opponents in Parliament, the Commons voted Byron out of his command. When he refused to abandon the Tower, Philip Skippon, an old soldier who had served in the Dutch army and who had recently been appointed to command the Trained Bands, was ordered to blockade the Tower — and if possible, capture it. But Skippon failed in his attempt to take it by surprise.

Byron, however, was in an impossible situation. The tradesmen of London refused to supply him with provisions; the merchants declined to send any bullion to the mint; Skippon's blockade by land was reinforced by a river blockade undertaken by the Thames watermen. Compelled to accept the fact that London was lost to the king's enemies, Byron beseeched Charles to set him free from his "vexation and agony" at the Tower. The king felt obliged to do so, and Sir John Conyers, a man acceptable to Parliament, took his place as lieutenant.

With the Tower lost, there was no hope of the royalists regaining London until the Parliamentary forces were defeated in the field. But it was the royalists themselves who were eventually defeated in the four-year Civil War. At Stowe-on-the-Wold, on March 26, 1646, the commander of the king's last army, Lord Ashley, sadly surrendered his sword to a soldier of Oliver Cromwell, who had emerged as the leader of the Roundheads. The Civil War was over and Parliament's control over London and the Tower was confirmed.

The office of lieutenant was vested in the Lord Mayor and that of constable in Sir Thomas Fairfax, commander in chief of Cromwell's New Model Army.

Charles fled to Scotland, but early in 1647 he was delivered back across the border to his enemies. In January 1649 the king was tried by a Parliamentary high court whose jurisdiction he vehemently denied, found guilty of treason, and executed at Whitehall. England thereupon entered into an eleven-year experiment with a republican form of government.

By the time of the restoration of the monarchy in 1660 — when the Prince of Wales, son of Charles I, was brought back from exile on the Continent to be proclaimed king as Charles II — not only had all the royal apartments at the Tower been demolished on orders of Cromwell's government, but the rest of the fabric had fallen badly into disrepair. The evil-smelling moat was soggy with sewage and the decomposing bodies of cats and dogs, while a jumble of decaying houses threatened to totter into it from the outer bank. But within a few months of Charles II's return, considerable sums had been spent upon improvements.

In June 1661 the diarist and minor government official Samuel Pepys, who occasionally enjoyed a merry dinner at the fortress with the new lieutenant, Sir John Robinson, was able to walk all the way around the inner and outer wards, which he did "with much pleasure." Five years later, however, in the summer of 1666, Pepys feared that the "fine Tower" which gave him that pleasure would be destroyed forever.

Pepys and his wife were in bed and asleep at three o'clock in the morning of September 2 when their maid Jane came into the room to tell them of a great

fire she had seen in the city. Pepys got out of bed, slipped on his nightgown, and went to look at it through the window of Jane's room. But he was not much impressed; he had seen many fires in his time and knew that they usually soon burned themselves out. He went back to bed and to sleep.

The next morning, however, Jane told her master that she had heard that three hundred houses had burned down in the night and that the fire was still raging around London Bridge. "So I made myself ready presently," he recorded in his diary, "and walked to the Tower; and there got up on one of the high places. Sir J. Robinson's little son going up with me; and there I did see the houses at that end of the bridge all on fire, and an infinite great fire on this and the other side the end of the bridge." When he had climbed down into the inner ward, Robinson told him that the fire had begun in a baker's house in Pudding Lane near London Bridge and that most of Fish Street had already been burned to the ground.

By midnight that Monday, the fire had consumed the whole of Thames Street, from Fresh Wharf to Puddle Dock, and had spread as far north as Cornhill, burning down the Elizabethan Royal Exchange and roaring west toward Cheapside. The next day St. Paul's Cathedral and the Guildhall, center of the city's government, were both burning fiercely, and the flames were leaping on past Newgate to the Temple. By Tuesday midnight the lead from the roof of the gutted St. Paul's was pouring down the streets like lava; and the Guildhall was still blazing like a torch "as if it had been a Palace of Gold, or a great building of burnished Brass." Newgate Prison, the Session House at the Old Bailey, and the Customs House were also in uncontrollable flames. Forty-four of the city companies' sixty livery halls had been effaced; eighty-seven of the city's ninety-seven parish churches and more than 13,000 houses had disappeared. No less than 395 acres of land lay utterly devastated under the choking smoke. In fact, the old city of London had been almost entirely burned away, and of its famous buildings only the Tower survived.

It seemed impossible on Tuesday night that even the Tower could survive. The flames had leaped across the Fleet Ditch and roared down into Fleet Street; and they were now threatening, in the blustering wind, to leap across the Tower moat as well.

In the earlier hours of the fire attempts had been made to check it by forming chains of fire fighters armed with leather buckets full of water, but the water merely hissed in the flames. The few, primitive fire engines that London then possessed had proved no more effective. Sir Thomas Bludworth, the hard-drinking vintner who was serving as Lord Mayor — when first called out to view the conflagration — had delivered himself of a contemptuous opinion: "Pish! A woman might pisse it out!" Later, he had been urged to order the wholesale pulling down of houses in the path of the fire, but he dared not give the order for fear of the claims of compensation that would ensue.

Yet it was soon clear enough that no other remedy would serve. The seamen brought up from the dockyards to act as fire fighters insisted that the only way to save what remained of the city was ruthlessly to blow up with gunpowder whole rows and streets of buildings and thus create an open gap so wide that no

Mr Everard imprifon'd in the Tower

burning embers could be thrown across it even by the strongest wind.

It was vital that action, however drastic, be taken to prevent the fire from reaching the Tower, for the fortress contained immense stores of the navy's gunpowder. If ignited, the gunpowder would cause an explosion of incalculable destructiveness, probably bringing down London Bridge and swamping every craft in the river. The explosion, the diarist and author John Evelyn thought, "would not only have beaten down and destroyed all the bridge; but sunk and torn all the vessels in the river, and rendered the demolition beyond all expression for several miles about the country."

At the last minute, the lieutenant ordered all the gunpowder to be removed. But even so, instructions had to be given for all the houses in Tower Street, as well as those adjoining the Tower, to be blown up. The subsequent deafening explosions led to panic among the crowds of terrified people flying from the flames. The cry went up that the cannon of the Tower were firing indiscriminately into the city; no regard was being paid to the lives of anyone. Every house within half a mile of the Tower, whether still occupied or not, was to be flattened so that the fortress itself could be saved. It was hours before the occupants of houses even as far away as Barking Alley could be persuaded that their lives were not in danger.

By then all the houses between the spreading fire and the Tower had been blown up and lay in flattened ruins under a cloud of dense, yellow smoke. But still the danger was not yet past. The Goldsmith's Company, which had earlier sent its treasures valued at

1,200,000 pounds into the Tower for safety, now ordered them to be brought out again and carried to Whitehall for fear that the heat would melt the precious metal. A detachment of soldiers formed a chain, and by the light of the flames the gold and silver plate, the bags of coins, and the medals were passed from hand to hand and stowed away into the hold of a boat anchored at Tower Wharf. The boat cast off as soon as the loading was completed and took the valuables away to the vaults of Whitehall Palace. The removal proved unnecessary; the demolition of the houses in Tower Street had saved the Tower and the blowing up of streets of houses elsewhere, combined with the merciful dropping of the wind at the same time, saved the rest of London.

Sir John Robinson, Lieutenant of the Tower at the time of the Great Fire, was a humane as well as a far-sighted man. During his period of office, his prisoners were treated as well as they had been for generations. Indeed, as the seventeenth century progressed, conditions at the Tower became comparatively comfortable for the majority of prisoners — and they were ever afterward to remain so. Jail fever, that virulent form of typhus, endemic in all other London prisons, was virtually unknown at the Tower even when it was filled to capacity after some plot or rebellion. It was also rare for a prisoner to be denied the use of his own furniture and books, the attention of his servants, the pleasures of meals provided by his own cook, the opportunity of receiving and sending as many letters as he cared to do, and the privilege of welcoming as many friends as chose to visit him.

When William Penn, the founder of Pennsylvania, was sent to the Tower in 1668 for the publication of an unlicensed religious tract, he was kept closely confined, but he was not prevented from writing his dissertation on the Christian duty of self-sacrifice, "No Cross, No Crown." When Samuel Pepys's friend Sir William Coventry was there in 1669 for challenging the Duke of Buckingham to a duel, he received so many visits from his friends that on some days there were as many as sixty coaches waiting outside the Tower gates. When Pepys himself was held there in 1679 on account of his alleged complicity in the Popish Plot, a stream of correspondence flowed in and out of his lodgings in a successful attempt to establish his innocence. And when the notorious Judge Jeffreys was there, having failed to escape to Hamburg disguised as a seaman after the deposition of his master James II in 1688, he was permitted to conduct as extensive a correspondence as Pepys had conducted and to receive as many visitors.

The hope of catching sight of such a famous face as that of Judge Jeffreys at one of the windows, or of seeing a celebrated figure walking along the battlements, was one of the reasons why the open spaces around the Tower were always crowded with sight-seers on a public holiday.

Another spectacle that frequently drew crowds to the Tower was the reception given to foreign ambassadors as they landed on Tower Wharf. In the reign of Charles II there was a particularly exciting reception when the Swedish ambassador landed in 1661. Since it was known that there had been an acrimonious dispute as to whether the French or the Spaniards should have precedence during the ceremony, the authorities had expected trouble on that occasion. The king, however,

had decided not to become involved in the dispute, and he informed the French and Spanish ambassadors that they must settle the quarrel for themselves. But he warned the Tower garrison to hold itself in readiness to intervene if this proved absolutely necessary.

The Spaniards arrived first on Tower Wharf; an observer counted fifty drawn swords around their ambassador's coach. But when the French appeared they were seen not only to be as heavily armed as the Spaniards but to outnumber them by four to one. Undaunted by this, the Spaniards — cheered on by the Londoners — attacked the French, cutting several of them to the ground and killing all their horses so that their ambassador's coach was brought to a standstill. In the subsequent affray several more Frenchmen and an almost equal number of Spaniards were killed, and an English onlooker was shot by a stray bullet. It was the Spaniards who gained the day in the end; and their ambassador's coach at last came down onto Tower Wharf to take up what he considered to be his rightful place as the doyen of the diplomatic community, the representative of Europe's foremost monarch.

The reception of foreign ambassadors did not normally supply such powerful entertainment as this. But there was nearly always something interesting to watch in the neighborhood of the Tower as when, for instance, a caravan of wagons wound their way toward the gates bringing in a load of treasure for safekeeping within the vaults. Early in the eighteenth century a procession of no less than fifty-five wagons, escorted by a strong guard of sailors, was to be seen toiling up the hill, carrying the wealth of gold and other precious metals captured on the high seas by the highly success-

ful privateers the *Frederick* and the *Duke*.

Regularly on November 5, the anniversary of the arrest of Guy Fawkes, crowds collected to watch the burning of his effigy on a huge bonfire outside the Tower. On that day there was also a thrilling display of fireworks, which were set off to the accompanying boom of cannon firing from the White Tower and Tower Wharf. There were also celebrations with bonfires, fireworks, and cannon, on the occasion of the king's birthday when, as the constable was informed by his deputy on that day in 1772, "the garrison was paraded; the guns on the Wharf and those on the ramparts were fired all round; all the warders attended in their new clothes, and at night [there was] a bonfire on the Hill and the whole garrison gave three volleys of shot. The warders had wine allowed 'em to drink the King's health, and the soldiers two barrels of beer. . . . Mr. D'Oyly gave all the officers a very handsome entertainment at his house in the evening."

The king's birthday celebrations did not always pass off so happily; often there were disturbances, and once, in June 1763, there was a serious riot. The crowds that collected to see the fireworks that year were even larger than usual. So great was the pressure on the fencing that enclosed an open well that the rails broke, and numerous people fell in. Six of them were drowned or crushed to death in the panic that followed, and nearly twenty were seriously hurt.

While the rescue operations were in progress, a sailor had his pocket picked by a Jew who was caught and thrown by the mob into the Tower moat. Protesting that he had broken his leg, the Jew hobbled out of the moat, and the crowd — deciding that he had therefore suffered punishment enough — allowed him to be carried off by a friend. He had not gone far, however, before he was seen to be walking quite normally beside his friend. The people thereupon ran after him with shouts and curses and chased him into the Jewish quarter near the old synagogue in Duke's Place. There the crowds were held at bay for a time by the inhabitants of the ghetto. But reinforced by sailors from the ships in the river, the mob soon broke through the barricades and rampaged through the streets. Several houses were broken into — their interiors ransacked, the wainscotting, doors, and window-frames pulled out, the windows smashed, and all the contents, including three children sick with smallpox, thrown out into the street. It was several hours before troops called out from the Tower were able to restore order to the ghetto.

These troops from the Tower were frequently needed, for the people who congregated in the area around the old fortress were notoriously unruly. There were numerous brothels there and scores of rowdy taverns. It was a favorite haunt of demagogues, who stood on upturned carts to harangue the passing crowds. It was an established rendezvous for demonstrators, and for unemployed and dissatisfied workmen, particularly coal heavers and underpaid seamen who regularly gathered on its slopes to protest against their low rates of pay and the poor conditions in which they had to live.

Riots were common. In the Gin Riots, huge mobs roared over Tower Hill threatening destruction to all in authority. In the Gordon Riots of 1780, drunken gangs roaring their hatred of Roman Catholics and Irishmen stormed around the Tower; and one of them, led by two wild prostitutes and a one-armed soldier, banging fire tongs and frying pans, ringing bells, and waving flags, attacked a tavern kept by a foreign Catholic and pulled it to the ground. The soldier and the two viragos were arrested, tried, and quickly hanged on a temporary gallows on Tower Hill on July 11, 1780. They had the distinction of being the last persons to be executed there.

A few years later the last attempt was made to take the Tower by force, when armed supporters of the violent radical group known as the Spenceans marched up to the gates, with banners flying and drums beating, to demand the surrender of the fortress in the name of the people. The guard listened in silence to their request, then burst out laughing in their faces. The people, as he well knew, were no longer interested in occupying the Tower. They were more attracted to spending their holidays visiting the historic fortress and enjoying the sights it had to offer.

VI

MENAGERIE, MINT AND MUSEUM

By the middle of the eighteenth century the Tower of London had become one of England's most popular destinations for a day's outing. Citizens and apprentices, servant girls and shop boys crowded there on public holidays; families from the provinces put it at the top of their lists of sights; foreign tourists considered it an essential part of their visit to England. For it was not only one of the great fortress prisons of Europe, it was one of its finest and oldest museums — and it contained one of Europe's best menageries.

There had been a menagerie in the Tower at least since the thirteenth century, when Frederick II of Germany sent a present of three leopards to Henry III. Soon afterward these leopards were joined by several lions, a bear, and an elephant — the latter, a present from the King of France, "a huge animal that was landed to the great astonishment of the people" who crowded to the Tower from all over England to see it. The king gave orders for a great house, twenty feet by forty feet, to be built for the elephant. In a document dated 1252 the sheriffs of London were required to pay four pence a day, and to provide a muzzle and chain, for the maintenance of a polar bear, which was trained to catch fish in the Thames. The cost of the upkeep of these various animals eventually grew considerable. In the reign of Edward II (1307–27) the lions were consuming a quarter of a sheep each day, and for the purchase of their food, the leopards were allowed sixpence a day — at a time when the human prisoners were allowed but a penny.

With each passing reign there were more and more animals in the keeping of the menagerie's custodian, the Master of the King's Bears and Apes. In the reign of

Queen Elizabeth I a German visitor found "all variety of creatures in the Tower including three lionesses, one lion of great size called Edward VI from his having been born in that reign; a tyger; a lynx; a wolf excessively old; this is a very scarce animal in England, so that their sheep and cattle stray about in great numbers, free from any dangers, though without anybody to keep them; there is besides, a porcupine, and an eagle. All these creatures are kept in a remote place, fitted up for the purpose with wooden lattices at the Queen's expense."

Both the bears and the lions were used for court entertainments, particularly so in the reign of James I whose passion for animal baiting was scarcely less than pathological. In the summer of 1604 King James, accompanied by the Duke of Lennox and some other favorite courtiers, went to the Tower and arranged for a lion and a lioness to be brought out of their cages and for a live cock to be thrown to them "which, being their natural enemy, they immediately killed and sucked the blood." Next a young lamb was thrown into the pit, yet this the lions "did not offer to hurt," so a fresh and supposedly more ferocious lion was brought in. Two mastiffs were set upon this new lion, which tossed one after the other out of the pit. Then one of the courtiers had the idea of throwing a spaniel into the ring to see what the lion would do to that. But the lion looked at the spaniel with a kind of morose affection and did nothing. Afterward the two animals lived together "in perfect amity for several years."

King James was further disappointed by a subsequent baiting at the Tower which was attended also by the Prince of Wales and Queen Anne. One of the bears in the menagerie, having killed a child, was condemned to be executed by a lion; but neither the first lion that was brought out to kill it nor any of the others that were afterward urged on to carry out the punishment could be persuaded to attack the bear. So the king had to content himself with the more common spectacle of a baiting to death by dogs.

Even before the lions and leopards came to the Tower in the thirteenth century, the historic fortress had its ravens. Perhaps the ungainly birds had always been there, for long before the Norman Conquest ravens were common in the streets of London where they were valued and protected as scavengers that picked up fish-bones and offal from the gutters. The ravens are still there now, carefully tended in a cage near the Lanthorn Tower, from which they fly to hop about on the lawns. Each of them is provided with a weekly allowance of three shillings worth of horseflesh; for there is a legend of unknown antiquity that once the ravens leave it, the Tower is doomed to fall — and with the Tower, all of England.

In the eighteenth century, the by-now frequent visitors would go from the menagerie on to the mint, an immense room with a flagstone floor and iron-barred windows, crowded with men at work around the rolling mills. Since the Norman Conquest, coins of the realm had been minted in the Tower in every reign except those of Richard I and Edward V. In the reign of Edward II a law was passed that all English moneys, wherever they were coined, should be made "in the same manner as in the Tower." In no reign, however, had there been more expert medalists working there than in that of Charles II, who upon his restoration to the

throne in 1660, brought over to England John Rotier, the greatest craftsman of his time. Rotier, one of three brothers eventually to be appointed to the Tower Mint, was the son of an Antwerp jeweler who had lent money to Charles II in his exile and had, in return, been promised employment for his sons when the time came for the English king to return to his throne.

Rotier's most distinguished predecessor at the mint had been the French engraver Nicholas Briot. Briot had fled to England from France, where his improved mechanical processes for the manufacture of coins had encountered the opposition of the reactionary officials of the Cours des Monnaies. In England, Briot had been kindly received by Charles I, who recognized the importance of his machinery and granted him "full power and authority to frame and engrave the first designs and effigies of the King's image in such size and forms as are to serve in all sorts of coins of gold and silver." In 1633 he was appointed chief engraver to the English mint where his machinery was shortly installed.

Briot's machinery was still in use when John Rotier was invited to work at the mint in 1661. The chief medalist at this time was Thomas Simon, a former pupil of Briot's, who did not take kindly to the foreigner's arrival. When Rotier's designs for a silver crown were chosen instead of those he submitted, Simon left the mint in anger.

From the time of Simon's departure until the death of Charles II in 1685, John Rotier and his brothers produced a stream of beautiful coins, seals, and medals. Their designs were especially gratifying to the king when — on introducing the figure of Britannia into the coinage (the figure that can still be seen on the British 50p piece) — they used as a model Charles's beautiful mistress Frances Stuart, Duchess of Richmond.

In March 1666 Samuel Pepys went to the Tower with Lord Brouncker to "see the famous Engraver, to get him to grave a seal for the office." "Did see," Pepys continued in his journal, "some of the finest pieces of work, in embossed work, that ever I did see in my life, for fineness and smallness of the images thereon. Here I also did see bars of gold melting, which was a fine sight." A few years later Pepys's fellow diarist John Evelyn, a close friend of the Master of the Mint, "went to the Tower to try a metal at the Assay-master's which only proved sulphur; then saw Monsieur Rotière, that excellent graver belonging to the Mint, who emulates even the ancients in both metal and stone; he was now moulding a horse for the King's statue, to be cast in silver, of a yard high."

Exquisite as was his workmanship, Rotier fell into disfavor after Charles's successor, James II, fled from England during the bloodless revolution of 1688. For Rotier was a "violent papist" and a suspected Jacobite (a partisan of the ousted James II), and he refused to acknowledge the sovereignty of the new Protestant king, William III. In January 1696 it was discovered that dyes from the coins of Charles II and James II had been abstracted from the mint by laborers who had handed them over to coiners in the Fleet prison, where guineas had been struck on gilded blanks of copper. Rotier, responsible for the custody of the dyes, was held to blame by a committee of the House of Commons and was removed from his office and from his house in the Tower.

Although security precautions at the Tower Mint

James I, who took savage delight in baiting the jungle cats in the Tower menagerie, would have been delighted by the delicately colored engraving at left, which pictures a tiger and his mate mauling an outclassed lion. Commoners were admitted to the zoo in increasing numbers after 1800, and according to a mid-century account, gullible bumpkins were often duped into buying tickets (right) for "the annual washing of the lions" — held on April Fool's Day.

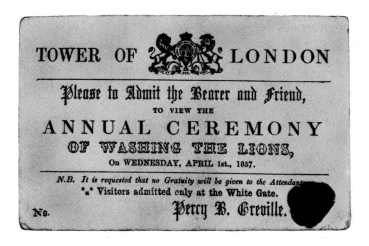

TOWER OF LONDON

Please to Admit the Bearer and Friend,

TO VIEW THE

ANNUAL CEREMONY

OF WASHING THE LIONS,

On WEDNESDAY, APRIL 1st, 1857.

N.B. It is requested that no Gratuity will be given to the Attendant.

⁎ Visitors admitted only at the White Gate.

No.

Percy B. Greville.

appear to have been extremely haphazard, no attempt to rob it was made until 1798. One morning in December of that year James Turnbull and a fellow workman named Dalton, having been sent off to have their breakfasts at the usual hour, returned unexpectedly, pistols in hand, and demanded of one of the manager's apprentices the key to the cupboard where the newly coined guineas were kept. Nearly paralyzed with fear, the apprentice handed the key over immediately. The two workmen then unlocked the cupboard, removed the 2,308 guineas that it contained, and pushed the terrified apprentice inside in their place. Neither man, however, got very far with his loot. Dalton was soon arrested in London, and Turnbull was captured while attempting to board a French packet on the coast.

The mint was removed from the Tower buildings to a new workshop on Tower Hill at the beginning of the nineteenth century, but the Royal Armouries, the oldest museum in England, still remain within the Tower's walls. Many of the exhibits were collected by Henry VIII, whose interest in armor was expert and intense and whose own suits were — and still are — on display. Married women in the seventeenth and eighteenth centuries crowded around these suits to stick pins into the padded codpieces, for old wives said that this was a well-attested way of ensuring conception.

Henry's armor was of plate, but before his time men wore mail, a protective covering of interlinked and riveted iron rings. This was the armor that the Roman cavalryman had worn after the introduction of the stirrup from the East had made it possible for him, thus heavily weighted, to maintain his balance in the saddle when rocked by a heavy blow. This was also

the armor — as can clearly be seen from the Bayeux tapestry — that both the English and the Normans wore at the Battle of Hastings.

Both armies at Hastings fought mainly with swords, lances, and battle-axes, the traditional weapon of the Saxon race. The English shield, which had been used by the Saxons for centuries, was heavy and round with a pointed boss in its center. The Normans used a longer, narrower, kite-shaped shield less cumbersome for a horseman.

The advent of heraldry had made European armor more decorative and colorful. Not only was a knight's shield painted with heraldic devices, but other parts of his armor, too, were embellished with colored symbols that established the particular distinction of his family. The emblems were repeated on the trapper of the horse and on the knight's linen surcoat, which, previously worn under his hauberk, or mail shirt, was now worn over it. In the thirteenth and early fourteenth centuries this surcoat was a loose, flowing robe that reached almost to the ankles, but the inconvenience of having a skirt of such length was sadly demonstrated in 1370 when Sir John Chandos, a gallant old knight and devoted friend of the Black Prince, dismounted from his horse to fight on foot on slippery ground, got his spurs entangled with his surcoat's hem, fell over, and was killed.

By that time mail armor was being replaced by plate. The disadvantage of mail was that it was not only extremely heavy but a violent blow could break the links and drive a chain of them deep into a gaping wound. On the contrary, plate, being inflexible, offered a smooth surface, which would deflect a glancing blow.

By the time of the battle of Agincourt in 1415, plate

107

had almost entirely taken the place of mail, which was then used only for interior gussets at armpits and elbows, and for tippets that gave extra protection around the neck between the back and breast-plates and the helmet. The conical helmet — more properly known as a basinet since the crested helmet was normally reserved for use in tournaments — left much of the face exposed; but instead of the fixed *nasar* covering the nose, which had been the only facial protection for the soldiers at the battle of Hastings, a movable visor was now fitted to the rim. This was either pivoted at the sides or hinged on the temple so that it could be pushed away from the face with a stroke of the back of the glove. When the knight was in battle, the visor was brought down over the eyes to provide as much protection as could be combined with reasonable vision. It was drawn into a point at the front so that a blow from a sword or lance would be the more easily deflected.

Over his armor the knight wore his *cote d'armes,* a loose emblazoned surcoat known also as a jupon. The garment was much shorter than the flowing robes that had led to the death of Sir John Chandos, though some old-fashioned knights, clinging to the styles of their ancestors, still wore their *cotes d'armes* with a trailing back. The baudrick, or ornamented sword belt, was tied around the hips. The hands were encased in inner gloves of velvet and outer gloves of hardened leather with overlapping steel plates and spikes of iron, called gadlings, on the knuckles. The shoulder reticulations were guarded by overlapping pauldrons and the armpits and elbow joints by circular palletes.

Putting on the padded undergarments and all these pieces of armor, their attachments and accessories, was a skilled and lengthy process. Each piece of harness had to be put on in a certain way and at a certain time, and if one piece went on in the wrong order it might not be possible to put on the others. The reticulated steel shoes, for example, had to go on before the leg guards, which fitted over the ankle.

Once the groom had equipped his master with a full suit of armor, fitted the poleyns, or knee guards, the lance rest, and the spurs — rowel spurs had replaced the pointed prick in the middle of the fourteenth century — the knight was weighed down by an immense encumbrance. Even raising a hand encased in gloves of velvet and boiled leather, with steel joints at the elbow and shoulder and thick rings of chain mail at the armpit, was a movement requiring some strength in itself. But walking about — let alone fighting — with the full weight of armor on the back, the basinet on the head, sword and dagger hanging from the belt, mace, axe, or lance in the hand, was an exertion that only the strongest men could make without soon becoming exhausted and that none could make with grace. The knight unfortunate enough to fall over thus encased found it extremely difficult, and sometimes on muddy ground impossible, to get up unless his page was there to help him. Otherwise he might lie for minutes on end, floundering on his back like a tortoise in its shell. Such was the fate at Agincourt of thousands of French knights who were caught struggling in the churned-up mud and were hacked to pieces with their own weapons by the unencumbered English archers.

Throughout the fifteenth century, then, the armorers of Europe endeavored to design suits of armor that would combine the greatest possible protection with the

most flexibility and the least weight. And nowhere in Europe were there to be found armorers more skillful than those of Milan and of the centers of the German craft at Nürnberg and Augsburg. Eighteenth-century visitors to the Tower of London could see, as can tourists today, as fine examples of such Italian and German masterpieces as were ever made. This armor is known as "Gothic" because the German master armorers were striving in their designs for something more than graceful practicality; they were attempting to reproduce in miniature the architectural motifs of their time.

With the development of artillery and of a new type of warfare in the sixteenth century, armor became more and more decorative as it became less and less practical. "Gothic" armor gave way to a more elaborate and ornate style that reflected the taste of the Italian Renaissance. Suits and helmets had become elaborately chiseled and were etched with acid, embossed and damascened with gold. Breastplates and leg pieces were almost skintight, following the curves of the body as though designed by the most expert tailors. The polished plates were nipped in at the waist, and billowed over the hips like a doublet. So highly decorated were their surfaces that they no longer offered a glancing surface to the point of the enemy's sword or lance; but by then protection was less their purpose than show.

A finely wrought suit was evidence of a man's worth and rank; it added an aura of martial magnificence to a portrait of its wearer by Titian or Holbein; it richly enhanced the appearance of such noblemen and courtiers as endeavored to impress each other upon the Field of Cloth of Gold, where Henry VIII met the French king in 1520. To make suits worthy of his magnificent

Wearing a closed casque much like the one at right, Henry VIII gallops down a jousting field on a heavily caparisoned black steed. Both monarch and mount wear the monogram of the king's first wife — a K, for the contemporary spelling of Catherine. The queen and her ladies sit in a palisaded box adorned with Tudor roses and Henry's own emblem, the cross-hatched portcullis.

presence and of his prowess on the tourney ground, Henry established an armory on the grounds of his palace at Greenwich. He staffed it with foreign craftsmen, mostly German, but it soon developed an immediately recognizable national style of its own. A characteristic example, still to be seen in the Tower, is the armor of Robert Dudley, Earl of Leicester, made at the Royal Workshops in Greenwich about 1585.

By then, however, the Greenwich armory and the armorers' craft were approaching their decline. When James I, the most unwarlike of men, succeeded Queen Elizabeth in 1603, the tournament was doomed, and the use of defensive armor in battle was soon to be abandoned too. In the Civil War (1642–46), although pikemen still wore breast and backplates, short tassets to cover the thigh, and broad-rimmed pot helmets, musketeers usually dispensed with armor.

After the Civil War, soldiers virtually abandoned the use of armor altogether. In the Seven Years' War (1756–63) the Tower of London was called upon to supply breastplates for the English cavalry sent out to fight in Germany, but by then armor was rarely worn except by a man sitting for a portrait to be hung beside those of his ancestors. The infantry officer went into battle with no more than a small gilt crescent dangling at the throat of his uniform, the shrunken symbol of the great, shining gorget worn by his predecessors, the sole remnant of their armor.

As well as containing the national museum of defensive armor, the Tower in the eighteenth century also held a magnificent collection of offensive weapons, illustrating their development from the swords, lances, and battle-axes of the Normans to — a later addition —

the cannon and mortar used against the French in the Napoleonic Wars. This collection was divided into four classes: the *arme blanche* (sword and dagger), the staff weapons (lance, spur, pike, axe, bill, and halberd), the arms of percussion (club, mace, and flail), and finally the projectile weapons (long bow, cross bow, javelin and sling, and firearms from pistol to cannon).

Visitors could see swords of the tenth to the fifteenth centuries, rapiers of the sixteenth and seventeenth centuries, the big two-handed, double-edged claymores of the Scottish Highlands, the huge lance that belonged to Henry VIII's friend the Duke of Suffolk. They could see "Henry VIII's Walking Staff" — a spiked club with three pistol barrels in the head — stone shot of the sixteenth century, and an immense mortar used at the siege of Namur in 1797. There, too, were ships' cannon dredged from the wrecks of the *Mary Rose,* sunk in action against the French in 1545, and of the *Royal George,* sunk by accident with all hands in 1782. There was also a variety of strange weapons brought back from the Orient and arranged around the armor of an Indian elephant, once the property of Lord Clive and brought by him, it was supposed, from the field of Plassey. All these items, and many more, may still be seen.

Yet of all the fascinating collections in the Tower none has ever aroused more interest than the crown jewels and royal regalia. These have been housed in the Tower ever since the beginning of the fourteenth century, after one of the most successful robberies in the history of crime was committed in London. It occurred in the year 1303, when King Edward I was away in the north fighting the Scottish rebels. A gang of robbers smashed down a wall of Westminster Abbey, broke their way into the Royal Treasury, and escaped with treasure worth 100,000 pounds — twice as much as the entire annual revenue of the kingdom. The Abbot of Westminster and several of the monks were arrested on charges of complicity and imprisoned in the Tower, but nothing could be proved against them and the robbers themselves were never caught. The stolen treasure, including many of the king's jewels, was never recovered.

It was thereupon decided that the Royal Treasury should be transferred to the Tower. In the reign of Henry III (1216–72) a small Jewel House had already been built within the walls of the fortress to contain and safeguard certain pieces of the royal treasure and regalia. And as the years passed, more valuables and regalia were accumulated there until the losses incurred in 1303 had been made good and the Tower became the repository of one of the most precious collections of jewels in all Europe. Time and again the kings of England were driven to despoil the collection when ambition, inclination, or necessity led them into war. For the cost of war, even in the fourteenth century, was immense, and it was only by pawning the royal treasure that the money could be raised.

In the fourteenth century a system to raise an army by contract was developed. Contracts were made with nobles, knights, or esquires who undertook to enlist an agreed number of armored men-at-arms and archers. The king, in turn, undertook to reimburse those who entered into contract with him as soon as the profits of war — in particular the ransoms paid by the families of rich prisoners — enabled him to do so. He also undertook to provide transport, both on the outward and return journeys, for each contracting noble, knight, and esquire, and for his retinue, baggage, and horses. To pay for this transport and to find the adequate security demanded by the contracting officers, the king was obliged to pledge his most valuable possessions.

While preparing for the expedition against the French that resulted in his astonishing victory at Agincourt, Henry V, for example, was compelled to pawn nearly all the crown jewels, and when these had been committed, to offer even the vestments and reliquaries of the Chapel Royal. Several of his crowns were pawned and one at least was broken up so that pieces of it could be distributed as pledges to various nobles who had undertaken to contribute troops to the king's army.

Despite the frequent spoliation of the crown jewels, however, and despite the fact that many of them were damaged or lost in war — a bejeweled gold fleuron was struck off the crown that Henry V wore around his helmet during the battle of Agincourt — the value of the collection continued to rise over the centuries. An inventory of the treasures of the Jewel House made in the reign of James I (1603–25) lists an amazing number of priceless crowns, circlets, coronets, scepters, rings, bracelets, and jeweled swords. No less than fifteen gold collars are described, all of them set with precious stones; while the "crowne imperyall of golde" — one of numerous crowns recorded — contained nineteen "greate pointed dyamondes, and betweene everye dyamonde a knott of perles, rubies and emeralds."

The royal regalia in the early seventeenth century also included a sapphire that was originally set into a ring worn by Edward the Confessor at his coronation

in 1043; a huge ruby given to the Black Prince, son of King Edward III, in the fourteenth century; a pearl-encrusted, heavily gilt silver spoon over a thousand years old; a sacred golden vessel (known as an ampulla) in the shape of an eagle, which was used at the coronation of Henry IV in 1399; and the beautiful pearl earrings worn by Elizabeth I.

Of all this immensely valuable and ancient collection, only the spoon, the ampulla, the sapphire, the ruby, the queen's pearls, and a few other precious stones now remain. For after the execution of Charles I in 1649, the Commonwealth government decreed that all the insignia of English royalty should be sold or destroyed. It was an act of vandalism that profited the government little, as the sale realized only a few hundred pounds. King Alfred the Great's gold crown, decorated with precious stones and little bells, brought no more than 248 pounds, 10 shillings; and the eleventh-century crown of Queen Edith was sold for only 16 pounds. The ampulla and spoon escaped, presumably because their uses in the coronation ceremony were not realized; and Edward the Confessor's sapphire, the Black Prince's ruby, and Queen Elizabeth's pearls were eventually recovered. But the rest of the collection disappeared forever; and most of the regalia that one can see in the Jewel House today dates from the time of the restoration of King Charles II.

Many of the pieces — some of them subsequently re-modeled for later monarchs — were made for Charles's coronation in 1661 and have been used in every coronation ceremony since. Two of the most valuable are the Imperial Crown of State and St. Edward's Crown.

The Crown of State contains the principal jewels

that survived the Commonwealth: Edward the Confessor's sapphire, the Black Prince's ruby, and Queen Elizabeth's pearls. The sapphire, set at the top of the crown as the centerpiece of a Maltese cross, was buried with Edward the Confessor in Westminster Abbey in 1066. The shrine was broken open in 1101 and the treasures in it were removed, the sapphire being used as the main stone in a crown made for Henry I. The ruby, set in the very center of the Crown of State, was given to the Black Prince by Don Pedro, King of Castile, in token of gratitude for the help the prince's knights gave to the Castilian army at the battle of Navaretto in 1367. Its long history is a particularly dramatic one.

The ruby had once belonged to the King of Granada, whom the ferocious Don Pedro had murdered. After the death of the Black Prince it came into the possession of Richard II, who seems to have had it in his keeping when he surrendered to the future Henry IV at Flint in 1399. Henry's son, Henry V, certainly wore it in his crown during the battle of Agincourt; and Richard III wore it in his at the battle of Bosworth Field. It was almost lost at Bosworth when Richard was killed and his crown, concealed in a hawthorn bush, was retrieved by supporters of the Earl of Richmond. Richmond used this crown to declare himself Henry VII, the first of the Tudor kings.

Immediately beneath the historic ruby, in the wide jeweled band that forms the base of the Imperial Crown of State, is an enormous diamond, the multi-faceted Second Star of Africa, which was cut from the famous Cullinan Diamond, the largest diamond ever mined. There are 2,782 other diamonds in the crown,

17 sapphires, 11 emeralds, 5 rubies, and 277 pearls, including Queen Elizabeth's 4 large pearls, which hang from the intersection of the two arches.

Loaded as it is with so many precious stones, the Crown of State is not as heavy as St. Edward's Crown. This crown is the one actually used during the coronation ceremony and takes its name from the traditional pledge that the new sovereign makes to govern England in accordance with the old laws of Edward the Confessor. It is of gold encrusted with diamonds, rubies, emeralds, sapphires, and pearls; and it has been used to crown every sovereign since Charles II — except the eighteen-year-old Queen Victoria, for whom it was considered too heavy. Victoria was crowned with the lighter Crown of State, which was specially remodeled for her, and St. Edward's Crown was carried throughout the ceremony by the Lord High Steward.

The coronation of Queen Victoria in 1838 was performed in accordance with a ceremony that had remained virtually unchanged for centuries and remains unchanged today.

The Great Sword of State, the Sword of Justice, and the Sword of Mercy are all carried before the new sovereign as he enters Westminster Abbey. A jeweled sword, one of the attributes of knighthood, is girt about the new sovereign during the ceremony as the Archbishop of Canterbury exhorts him to use it to do justice, stop the growth of iniquity, protect the holy Church of God, help and defend widows and orphans, restore the things that are gone to decay, maintain the things that are restored, punish and reform what is amiss, and confirm what is in good order. The jeweled sword is then unbuckled and placed upon the altar alongside the other attribute of knighthood, the golden spurs.

One by one, the other pieces of the royal regalia are brought forward to play their respective parts in the ancient ceremony: the Orb, a golden globe surmounted by a diamond-studded cross, symbolic of the world ruled by the emblem of Christianity; the Royal Sceptre with the Cross, symbol of royal power and justice; the Rod with the Dove, ensign of the monarch's duty as guardian and guide of his people; the Armills, bracelets signifying sincerity and wisdom; the Coronation Ring, indicative of kingly dignity; the Ampulla in which the holy oil is contained; the Anointing Spoon with which the oil is applied to the sovereign's head, breast, and palms.

All these pieces are of gold, richly encrusted with precious stones. The Royal Sceptre with the Cross, for example, is a golden staff three feet in length studded with diamonds and rubies. It contains, in addition to a huge amethyst and a magnificent emerald, the largest cut diamond in the world.

Numerous as these pieces are, they form only a small part of the treasures guarded in the Jewel House. There are several crowns there, apart from the Imperial Crown of State and St. Edward's Crown. One of the most splendid of these is the crown made for Queen Elizabeth, the queen mother. This contains the legendary Indian diamond known as the Koh-i-noor, the Mountain of Light, whose history can be traced back to the thirteenth century. Five hundred years later it passed into the hands of the East India Company, which presented it to Queen Victoria in 1850. The tradition is that it brings good luck to any woman

By the King.
A PROCLAMATION
For the Difcovery and Apprehenfion of *John Lockier, Timothy Butler, Thomas Blood*, commonly called Captain *Blood, John Mafon*, and others.

who wears it, but ill fortune to any man. Certainly many of the men who have owned it in the course of its long history have met a violent death.

There are also several scepters (in addition to the two held by the monarch, one in each hand, at his coronation), a Queen's Orb as well as a King's Orb, five Swords of State, ten silver-gilt Maces (used as ceremonial staffs by the king's officers), sixteen State Trumpets of silver, and a wonderful variety of sacramental and banqueting plate, used for the administration of the sacraments in the coronation service and at the great banquets that follow it.

The oldest of the banqueting plate is the Elizabethan salt cellar of 1572. All the other pieces were made after the restoration of the monarchy, the two largest having been given to Charles II on the occasion of his accession by the cities of Exeter and Plymouth. The present from Exeter is a salt cellar adorned with precious stones in the form of a Norman keep. The one from Plymouth is an elaborate container for warm and scented water in which the guests at the banquet could rinse their cutlery or their fingers.

It was soon after these two precious pieces had passed into the royal collection that Thomas Blood, a self-styled colonel, made his extraordinary and almost successful attempt to steal the crown jewels. Blood was a notorious desperado whose grandfather, an English army officer, had settled in Ireland where he had been elected Member of Parliament for Ennis. Thomas was born in Ireland in about 1618 and, through his father's influence, had become a Justice of the Peace at the age of twenty-one. During the Civil War between Parliament and the royalists he had, with characteristic op-

portunism, fought first on one side, then on the other. Contriving somehow to be on the winning side when the war was over, he was rewarded with confiscated royalist lands. In 1650 Blood married the daughter of a well-to-do Lancashire landowner, and his future seemed happily assured. But at the restoration of King Charles II in 1660 his estates, in turn, were confiscated by the Court of Claims, and embittered and penniless, as he put it himself, he embarked upon the life of an adventurer. It was a life that he was never afterward to abandon.

In 1663 Blood was implicated in a daring plot to seize Dublin Castle. After the plot's failure, he escaped from the authorities and roamed about Ireland in a variety of disguises before settling down in Holland and then in England, where he succeeded in passing himself off as a doctor. In 1670 he and some companions made an unsuccessful attempt to kidnap and hold for ransom the Duke of Ormonde, the Lord High Steward. But having failed to retrieve his fortunes this way, he conceived an even more daring crime — the theft of the crown jewels.

At that time the crown jewels were kept in a cupboard behind a wired grille in the basement of the Martin Tower. They were in the custody of the Assistant Keeper of the Jewels, Talbot Edwards, an ex-soldier of seventy-six who lived with his wife and daughter on the upper floors of the Martin Tower. Since his meager salary was so often in arrears, Edwards had sought and obtained permission from Gilbert Talbot, Keeper of the Jewels, to show the collection to visitors for a fee.

One day in April 1671 an aged, bearded clergyman

Shakespeare's friend and patron, the Earl of Southampton, was confined to the Tower in 1601 for his part in the abortive Essex Rebellion. The young peer celebrated his release two years later by sitting for a portrait (above) that included an inset view of the White Tower (top).

in the robes of a doctor of divinity came to the Tower and asked if he and his wife, an equally ancient lady, could see the crown jewels. Granted permission to do so, the couple was conducted to the Martin Tower where the old lady, upon sight of such valuable and mystical regalia, was seized with "a qualm upon her stomach." She prevailed upon Mr. Edwards to fetch her a glass of spirits. This was provided by Mrs. Edwards, who invited the clergyman's wife to her own private apartments where she could lie down and recover her strength upon a bed. The invitation was accepted; and when the lady and her husband departed some time later, they expressed themselves as being "very thankful for this civility."

Wishing to express his thanks in a more generous manner, the clergyman returned to the Tower a few days later with a present of several pairs of white gloves for Mrs. Edwards. These were accepted with delighted gratitude, and the clergyman was asked to call again whenever he felt so inclined.

The next time he did so he made some flattering remarks about Mrs. Edwards's daughter, such a "pretty gentlewoman"; and he mentioned that he had a nephew about her age, a young man with a handsome income of some two or three hundred pounds a year in land. "If your daughter be free," he added, "and you approve of it, I will bring him hither to see her, and we will endeavour to make it a match!"

Delighted by the prospect of so wealthy a son-in-law, Mrs. Edwards asked the clergyman to dinner. He accepted readily, said grace with deep piety, and offered up a prayer for the king and queen and all the royal family. After dinner, Edwards conducted his guest through the Martin Tower, pointing out its most notable antiquities. During the tour the clergyman expressed his admiration of a case of pistols: they were just the very articles to serve as a present for a young nobleman of his acquaintance, if Edwards could be persuaded to part with them for a consideration. Edwards readily agreed. And so, having arranged to return to the Tower with his nephew at seven o'clock on the morning of May 9, the clergyman departed.

Dressed once again in his clerical attire, his unprepossessing features disguised as before by a false white beard, Colonel Blood — for, of course, it was he — arrived at the Tower on the ninth. Blood was accompanied by his son, to act the part of the nephew, and by two others, introduced as friends of his who had a strong curiosity to see the crown jewels. All four men carried walking sticks with rapier blades concealed in the shafts, and all had daggers and pistols in their pockets.

His wife was on her way, Blood told Edwards, suggesting that they wait for her arrival before going upstairs to the ladies. In the meantime, perhaps his friends might see the jewels? Edwards was happy to oblige and conducted them downstairs. The young man remained outside; and Miss Edwards, dressed in her best clothes and excitedly looking down upon him from her upstairs window, supposed that he must be the young nephew, her intended bridegroom.

No sooner had Edwards reached the bottom of the steps that led down into the cellar than a cloak was thrown over his head and a gag pushed into his mouth: "a great plug of wood, with a small hole in the middle to take breath at, was tied on with a waxed leather which went round his neck. At the same time they fastened an iron hook to his nose that no sound might pass from him that way."

The conspirators told Edwards that no harm would come to him if he stayed quiet, but the brave old man refused to submit. He struggled to free himself and made as much noise as he could. His assailants gave him a few "unkind knocks" on the head with a wooden mallet until he fell to the ground, where he continued to struggle until one of the men stabbed him in the belly. "There," his attacker said, kneeling down beside his head and listening for the sounds of breathing, "he is dead. I will warrant him."

The three men then set about breaking into the cupboard where the jewels were kept. Blood got out a crown and stamped on it so that it could be more conveniently concealed under his cloak; one of the others picked up an orb and pushed it down his baggy breeches; the third put the Black Prince's ruby into his pocket and began to file a scepter in two.

Just at that moment Edwards's son arrived unexpectedly at the door of the Martin Tower. He had been abroad in the army for several years and was now on leave. Blood's son attempted to delay the young soldier at the door, but since this was his family's home he could not reasonably be prevented from entering it and going upstairs to see his mother and sister. As soon as he was out of sight, young Blood rushed down to warn his father what had happened.

The colonel and his accomplices emerged from the Martin Tower with the pieces of the regalia they had so far managed to steal from the cupboard hidden under their clothes. Walking as quickly as they dared, but not running for fear of arousing suspicion, they passed by the White Tower, then went through the gateway of the Bloody Tower and along the outer ward toward the Byward Tower. Before they had reached the Byward Tower, however, there were loud shouts behind them.

Edwards's son, having greeted his mother and sister, had gone downstairs to see his father whom he had discovered on the floor of the Jewel House, still alive but lying in a pool of blood. The alarm had been given and the pursuit began. The yeoman on guard at the gateway of the Byward Tower attempted to stop the four by-then running men with his halberd, but Blood let fly at him with his pistol and, followed by the others, raced out along the causeway toward the Middle Tower.

Instead of seeking safety by escaping through the Middle Tower, however, Blood and one of his accomplices turned to the left, jumped down onto Tower Wharf and pushed their way through the crowds along the river front. Shouting "stop thief" at the tops of their voices, they pointed to their pursuers as the villains. For a few moments it seemed that they might escape in the confusion they succeeded in causing, but they were soon overpowered and thrown into the dungeons, where their two companions shortly joined them. The benign old clergyman was seen to be, in fact, a beardless, tall, "rough-boned man, with small legs, a pock-frecken face with little hollow blue eyes." His features were "daring, villainous and unmerciful."

A pearl and a diamond had fallen out of their settings in the crown during "the robustious struggle." But both they and the Black Prince's ruby were eventually recovered and returned to the custody of Talbot Edwards, whose stalwart behavior was rewarded by a grant of 200 pounds. So delayed was the payment, however, that Edwards was obliged to sell his right to receive it at a discount of 50 per cent in order to pay his doctor's bill. He died soon afterward.

Colonel Blood fared much better. The king, intrigued by accounts of his exploit, wanted to meet the famous rogue. At the interview, Charles was evidently much taken with the colonel's outrageous charm and impudence, his disarming rascality; for Blood was not merely pardoned, but his lands were restored to him together with a pension of 500 pounds a year.

Such munificence naturally led to rumors that the king had all along been in league with Blood, that sorely pressed for money, he had proposed the theft to Blood so that the two of them might share the proceeds. Others held that the king, when drunk, had laid a bet that the crown jewels would be stolen and had put up Blood to win his wager for him. The truth was more prosaic. In return for his freedom, his lands, and his pension, the ingenious and daring colonel was to act as a spy for the government and the court, to spread rumors in the city when required to do so, and to inform against republicans and would-be traitors. He evidently found the bargain a satisfactory one, for a few days after it was concluded an acquaintance found Colonel Blood strutting about on Tower Green wearing a handsome new suit and periwig, "exceeding pleasant and jocose."

VII

THE TOWER ENDURES

Although its fine collections of armor and weapons and of jewels and royal regalia had made it one of the most celebrated museums in eighteenth-century Europe, the Tower of London remained England's principal state prison. In times of national unrest its cells and dungeons were as crowded as they had ever been in the days of the Tudors and Stuarts.

Charles II ruled for twenty-five years following the restoration of the monarchy in 1660, but his brother, the Roman Catholic King James II, proved to be an unpopular sovereign. Three years after his accession, James was overthrown in the bloodless revolution of 1688, and his Protestant daughter and her Dutch husband came to the throne as William and Mary. Their successor was Queen Anne, the younger daughter of James II. In 1714, upon the death of Anne, who outlived all her seventeen children, the crown devolved upon a German prince who became King George I of the House of Hanover. (See chart, page 168.)

The descendants of James II by a second marriage did not abandon their claims to the throne, however. In 1715 and again in 1745 the so-called Jacobites made unsuccessful attempts to oust the new German Protestant dynasty and to restore the Stuarts — and once more the Tower was filled with prisoners, this time the leaders of the defeated rebel armies.

In 1715 Sir James Radcliffe, third Earl of Derwentwater, was brought there after the surrender of the Jacobites at Preston and was lodged in the Devereux Tower together with the earls of Nithsdale and Carnwarth and lords Widdrington, Kenmure, and Nairn. Sir Robert Walpole, the prime minister, was offered 60,000 pounds to spare Derwentwater's life; but protesting that he was determined to make an example of the rebel leader, he advised King George not to give way to the pleas of the earl's numerous friends. Thus, Derwentwater, along with Kenmure, died on Tower Hill in February 1716, declaring his loyalty to the son of James II, the man he called King James III. He was but an early martyr in the cause for which so many other noble lords from the north were soon to die.

None died more bravely than the old Scottish lords Balmerino and Lovat, both of whom were taken prisoner in 1746 after the second defeat of the Jacobites at Culloden. Horace Walpole, son of the former prime minister, who was present at Lord Balmerino's trial, said that he was "the most natural brave old gentleman he had ever seen," and that at the bar of the court he "behaved himself like a soldier and a man." Refusing to admit that he had committed any crime and declining to sue for mercy, Balmerino was committed to the Tower, a plain, simple, and clumsy old man but one of such patent honesty and sincerity that "none could do other than admire him."

The only time Balmerino displayed any anger in the Tower was when the lieutenant told him that the time had been fixed for his execution. It was not that he was angry on his own account, but on that of his wife who was present having dinner with him and who rose to her feet in shock at the lieutenant's words. Balmerino gently reassured her, "Pray, my lady, sit down, for it shall not spoil your dinner." Then, turning to the lieutenant, he reprimanded him crossly with the words, "Lieutenant, with your damned warrant you have spoiled my lady's dinner."

When the day of execution came, Lord Balmerino behaved with astonishing calm. He talked cheerfully with his friends who had come to say good-by to him, took a glass of wine with them, and asked how his fellow Jacobite Lord Kilmarnock, who had been beheaded on Tower Hill earlier that morning, had conducted himself on the scaffold. When the lieutenant delivered him up to the under-sheriff for execution and concluded his remarks with the words "God bless King George," Balmerino admonished him with a stern voice and sterner look — "God bless King *James*." But then he turned back to his friends and said as lightly as though he were going to a tavern for his dinner, "Gentlemen, I shall detain you no longer."

He mounted the scaffold wearing the blue military coat, turned up with red and fastened with brass buttons, that he had worn at Culloden. "His countenance was serene," an eyewitness reported, "his air free and easy; he looked quite unconcerned, and like one going on to a party of pleasure, or some business of little or no importance." He walked several times around the scaffold, pausing now and again to bow to the people who had come to watch him die, carefully reading the inscription on his coffin, and examining the block — a better, smoother one than that provided for Lord Kilmarnock, who had required the executioner to plane the rough edges with the point of his axe.

He next asked for his spectacles so that he could read his speech to the spectators. When he had done so, the executioner came forward to ask his pardon. "Friend, you need not ask me for forgiveness," Balmerino answered him, "the execution of your duty is commendable." At these words the headsman, who had had to take a strong drink to prevent him from faint-

"At this sad scene which blood must deeply stain,
Scarce can the pitying Eye the Tear restrain"
begins the verse accompanying this contemporary
engraving of the execution of the Jacobite rebels
Balmerino and Kilmarnock. Thousands of curious
citizens thronged Tower Hill on August 18, 1746,
to witness the public beheading of the Scotsmen.

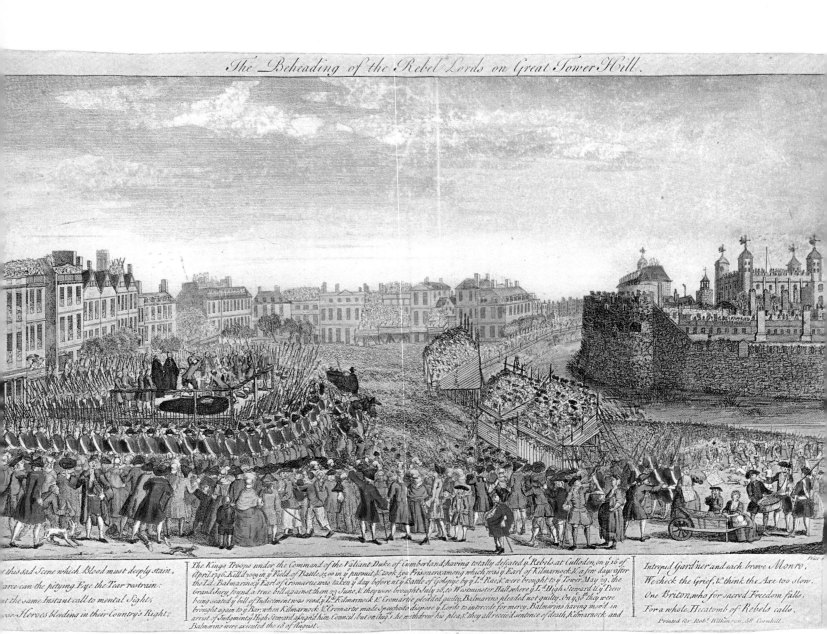

The Beheading of the Rebel Lords on Great Tower Hill.

t this sad Scene which Blood must deeply stain,
arce can the pitying Eye the Tear restrain:
t the same Instant call to mental Sight,
oo Heroes bleeding in their Country's Right:

The Kings Troops under the Command of the Valiant Duke of Cumberland, having totally defeated y Rebels at Culloden, on y 16 of April 1746, Kill'd 2000 in y Field of Battle & 500 in y pursuit & took 500 Prisoners, among which was y Earl of Kilmarnock & a few days after the Ld Balmarino & Earl of Cromartie was taken y day before at y Battle of Golspye by y Ld Rae, & were brought to y Tower May 29, the Grand Jury found a true bill against them 29 June, & they were brought July 28, to Westminster Hall where y Ld High Steward & y Peers being seated y bill of Indictment was read, y Ld Kilmarnock & Cromartie pleaded guilty, Balmarino pleaded not guilty. On y 30th they were brought again to y Bar, when Kilmarnock & Cromartie made Speech to dispose y Lords to intercede for mercy, Balmarino having mov'd in arrest of Judgment y High Steward assign'd him Council, but on Aug 1 he withdrew his plea, & they all receiv'd sentence of death, Kilmarnock and Balmarino were executed the 18 of August.

Intrepid Gard'ner and each brave Monro,
We check the Grief, & think the Axe too slow,
One Briton, who for sacred Freedom falls,
For a whole Hecatomb of Rebels calls.

Printed for Robt Wilkinson, 58 Cornhill.

ing before the execution of Lord Kilmarnock, burst into tears; and Balmerino slapped him on the back by way of encouragement. "Friend, I never was rich," he continued, taking three guineas out of his pocket, "this is all the money I have now, and I am sorry I cannot add anything to it except my coat and waist-coat," which he thereupon took off and placed on his coffin. He then took off his tiewig, put on a plaid cap, declared that he died a true Scotsman, and turning down the collar of his shirt indicated to the executioner the place where he should strike. "O Lord," he prayed, kneeling down at the block, "reward my friends, forgive my enemies, bless King James and receive my soul."

Finally, Balmerino gave the customary signal by letting his hands fall. But the "unexpected suddenness of the movement so surprised the executioner," an observer recorded, "that though he struck the part directed, the blow was not given with strength enough to wound him very deep; on which it seemed as if he made an effort to turn his head towards the executioner, and the under jaw fell and returned very quick, like anger and gnashing the teeth; but it could not be other wise, the part being convulsed. A second blow immediately succeeding, the first rendered him, how-ever, quite insensible, and a third finished the work. His head was received in a piece of red baize."

Soon after the execution of Lord Balmerino, the eighty-year-old Lord Lovat followed him to the scaffold and died with as little evident concern. Indeed, Lovat appeared quite cheerful on his last morning, sending his wig to the barber with instructions for it to be combed out genteelly and sitting down to a good break-fast of minced veal. He ordered coffee and chocolate for his friends whose health he himself drank in wine. When the sheriff came for him, he responded with alacrity, "I am ready"; and he walked with firm step to the scaffold.

An enormous crowd had assembled on Tower Hill to watch the execution, as though they knew that on this day — April 9, 1747 — they were to witness the death of the last man to be beheaded in England. "God save us!" exclaimed Lovat when he saw the immense num-bers of people. "Why should there be such a bustle about taking off an old grey head that cannot go up three steps without other bodies to support it?" So over-laden, in fact, was one of the spectators' stands over-looking the scaffold that a support cracked and broke, bringing it tumbling to the ground and crushing sev-eral people to death. "The more mischief, the better sport," Lovat grimly murmured.

As Lord Balmerino had done, Lovat inspected the inscription on his coffin and the edge of the axe. Noticing that the executioner appeared nervous and morose, he clapped him on the shoulder with the words, "Cheer up thy heart, man. I am not afraid. Why should you be?"

Crowds almost as enormous as those assembled on Tower Hill to witness Lovat's beheading came out again on May 5, 1760, to see Earl Ferrers ride out to his execution. Ferrers, who seems to have been suffer-ing from homicidal mania, had ordered his honest, hardworking steward to attend him one Friday after-noon at his country seat, Staunton Harold in Leicester-shire. There, under the misapprehension that the man "had combined with the trustees to disappoint him of a contract for coal-mines," he shot the steward as the man knelt before him on the carpet of his room. Upon his arrest, Lord Ferrers was conveyed to the Tower where, according to a contemporary account, he was lodged "in the round tower, near the drawbridge. Two wardens constantly attended in his room, and one waited at the door. At the bottom of the stairs two soldiers were placed, their bayonets fixed; and a third was stationed on the draw-bridge: and the gates of the Tower were shut an hour before the usual time, on the occasion of this imprisonment."

Although he displayed "evident proofs of discomposure of mind," Ferrers was found guilty of murder and was condemned to death. He appealed for the sentence to be carried out by beheading within the confines of the Tower; but this privilege was denied him, it being ruled that peers convicted of capital crimes must now die by hanging at Tyburn as was required of other criminals. So, on the day of his death, Lord Ferrers rode out of the Tower gate in his own landau drawn by six horses, attended by the chaplain of the Tower and the sheriff, dressed in a white suit richly embroidered with silver. On their slow way through the crowds of spectators, Lord Ferrers asked the sheriff if he had ever seen such a concourse of people collected together before: "the sheriff answered in the negative; to which the unhappy peer replied, 'I suppose it is because they never saw a lord hanged before.'"

Ferrers had been well treated in the Tower. His mistress, Mrs. Clifford, took lodgings in Tower Street so as to be near him, and she was allowed to send him a message every day and to receive one from him in return. He was even allowed to have visits from his four illegitimate children. In fact, Ferrers lived in a perfectly regular manner, it was reported at the time. "His breakfast consisted of a muffin, and a bason of tea with a spoonful of brandy in it. After dinner and supper he drank a pint of wine mixed with water."

Indeed, the Tower by then was agreed to be as comfortable a prison as could be found anywhere. Its inmates were treated with none of the harshness that had characterized the days of Waad and was still a feature of all the other prisons of London. When the radical demagogue John Wilkes was brought there three years after the death of Lord Ferrers for publishing a libelous issue of his newspaper, *The North Briton,* he was welcomed almost as an honored guest. And when John Wesley visited the eccentric anti-Catholic agitator Lord George Gordon after the no-popery riots in 1780, he found him comfortably installed in an apartment with "an abundance of books, enough to furnish a study."

To be sure, the dangerous prisoner Gordon had at first been kept in a "dark dirty little apartment" without books or pen. All incoming letters had been opened before being passed on to him, and he had been allowed no visitors other than members of his own family — and they had been permitted to stay for no longer than an hour, during which the jailers remained within earshot. But all these rules had soon been relaxed. Gordon was given permission to walk around the ramparts, to receive visitors in private, and to have meals sent in. John Wesley found that he had "no cause to complain of any person or thing."

Although the Tower was so much more comfortable than all the other prisons of London, it had one par-

ticular and discouraging disadvantage: escape from it was almost impossible.

Escapes certainly had been made in every century since Bishop Rannulf Flambard — under whose direction the White Tower had been finished in the reign of Henry I — had got away by means of a rope smuggled to him inside a wine cask. It was also by rope that two prisoners, who had been captured fighting on the royalist side in Ireland during the Civil War — Lord Macguire and Colonel MacMahon — had tried to escape in 1644. They succeeded in sawing through their prison door and in clambering down into the moat with a rope that they found in the Tower, following directions written on a piece of paper concealed inside a loaf of bread. The two also succeeded in swimming across the moat, but on the far side they were recaptured and sent back to their cells. Later, they were hanged at Tyburn.

Another royalist Lord Capel had also let himself down into the moat with a rope. He chose a time when the tide was at its lowest, as he could not swim and had to wade through from bank to bank. He was a very tall man but even so the stinking, glutinous water came up to his neck as his feet had sunk into the mud. Every step required an arduous effort, and by the time he reached the other side he was scarcely able to summon the effort to pull himself out. His friends were there to help him, however, and they spirited him away to chambers in the Temple, where he remained for three days before being taken across the river to Lambeth. Unfortunately, the waterman who rowed him across heard him addressed as "My Lord" and, suspecting the identity of his passenger, followed him

to the house where he was to be concealed. He went to the authorities and asked them what Cromwell's government would "pay to know the place Lord Capel lay." He settled for twenty pounds, and Capel was retaken and beheaded.

A few years later one of Capel's enemies in the Civil War Colonel John Lambert, who had been imprisoned in the Tower for opposing General Monck's plan for the restoration of Charles II, escaped as Capel had done, by letting himself down by rope into the moat. In order to gain time to make good his getaway, Lambert persuaded the woman who made his bed to climb into it wearing his nightcap and to draw the curtains. The warder, seeing the curtains drawn as he went on his rounds, said "Goodnight, my Lord," to which the old woman murmured a gruff reply. The kindly but simple-minded creature was still in bed when the warder made his early morning rounds. On drawing back the curtains, he exclaimed: "In the name of God, Joan, what makes you here? Where is my Lord Lambert?" "He is gone," she replied unconcernedly, "but I cannot tell you whither." Like Capel, Lambert was not free for long, however, and by the end of the month he was brought back to prison again.

After John Lambert's escape, security precautions at the Tower were tightened so that it was no longer possible to escape by rope as so many prisoners in the past had done; more devious methods were required. The problem was ingeniously solved in 1716 when the Jacobite Earl of Nithsdale got out of the Tower in the most dramatic escape ever attempted there.

As soon as she heard that her husband had been captured after the battle of Preston, taken to London,

On the night of October 30, 1841, a flash fire
erupted in the Bowyer Tower and rapidly spread
to the storehouses east of the Chapel of St. John.
Before the conflagration could be brought under
control, the White, Martin, and Brick towers had
been damaged and the Small Armouries (shown in
the 1841 engraving below) had been engulfed by
flames. Repairs began at once, and during the
reconstruction countless ordinary citizens — such as
those inspecting the gutted Brick Tower at left —
turned out to survey the damage.

and sentenced to be beheaded with other Scottish lords, Lady Nithsdale — although of a delicate constitution — immediately had a horse saddled and rode to Newcastle on a bitterly cold February day. From Newcastle she took the stagecoach to York, where she found that the departure of the mail coach for the south was held up by heavy snow. Fearful that she would be too late to save her husband's life, Lady Nithsdale decided to take to the saddle again, and she rode all the way to London. She dashed to St. James's Palace, pushed her way through the servants and attendants in the corridors and on the stairs, and found King George in an anteroom preparing to enter the drawing room.

"I threw myself at his feet," she recorded, "and told him in French [the German-born king understood only a few words of English] that I was the unfortunate Countess of Nithsdale. . . . But seeing that he wanted to go off without taking my petition, I caught hold of the skirt of his coat, that he might stop and hear me. He endeavoured to escape out of my hands, but I kept such a strong hold, that he dragged me on my knees, from the middle of the room to the very door of the drawing-room. At last one of the Blue Ribands who attended his Majesty took me round the waist, while another wrested the coat from my hands. The petition, which I had endeavoured to thrust into his pocket, fell to the ground in the scuffle, and I almost fainted away from grief and disappointment."

Lady Nithsdale soon recovered, however, and she promptly devised a plan to deliver her husband from the Tower herself since she could not get him pardoned by the king. Enlisting the help of her sympathetic landlady, Mrs. Mills, and that of her friend Mrs.

Morgan, she planned to free him in female disguise. She would take the two ladies to the Tower on the day before that fixed for her husband's execution, on the pretext of saying good-by to him. Since he was permitted no more than two visitors in his cell at a time, she would first take in Mrs. Morgan, who was to conceal about her person an extra dress of the same color and style as the one worn by Mrs. Mills. Lord Nithsdale was to put this dress on while Lady Nithsdale showed Mrs. Morgan to the door of the cell and asked her — in a voice loud enough for the guards in the room below to hear — to run as quickly as she could to fetch her maid, as Lady Nithsdale had an urgent, last-minute plea to submit to the king, and the maid was to take it to him.

Next, according to Lady Nithsdale's plan, Mrs. Mills was to be brought into the cell pretending to be in tears so that she would have an excuse for holding a handkerchief to her face and thus hiding it from the guards in the anteroom. Lord Nithsdale, by then already wearing the extra dress, was to put on Mrs. Mills's hood and leave wearing it together with "an artificial headdress of the same colored hair as hers." Lady Nithsdale had observed on previous visits that the guards were usually busy talking to their wives and daughters in the anteroom, and she trusted that they would not notice that two women had gone up but three had come down.

On the day chosen for the deception, Lady Nithsdale took first Mrs. Morgan, then Mrs. Mills, up the stairs to the cell as planned. Having helped her husband to dress and having put the wig and hood on his head, she painted over his eyebrows which were dark and

The rapidly restored Tower complex was a major
tourist attraction during the nineteenth century,
drawing sailors, artists, and casual sight-seers in
droves. This view from Tower Hill shows the
repaired White Tower and the Small Armouries
as they appeared a single year after the disastrous
fire that severely damaged the structure in 1841.

thick and "rouged his face and cheeks to conceal his beard which he had not had time to shave." Then, so she continued her account, "I went out leading him by the hand, whilst he held his handkerchief to his eyes. I spoke to him in the most piteous and afflicted tone, bewailing the negligence of my maid Evans, who had ruined me by her delay. Then I said, 'My dear Mrs. Betty, for the love of God, run quickly and bring her with you; you know my lodging, and if you ever made despatch in your life, do it at present; I am almost distracted with this disappointment.' The guards opened the door, and I went downstairs with him, still conjuring him to make all possible despatch. As soon as he had cleared the door, I made him walk before me, for fear the sentinel should take notice of his walk. . . . Everybody in the room, who were chiefly the guards' wives, and daughters, seemed to compassionate me exceedingly."

Lady Nithsdale then returned to the cell — where only the real Mrs. Mills was waiting — and while her husband made good his escape, she affected to talk to him, answering her own questions in an imitation of his voice, which she had been practicing. Then she opened the door of the cell and, leaving with Mrs. Mills, said good-by to the empty cell in a loud voice, remarking that she would have to go herself to find her maid, but that as soon as she had done so she would come back, or if the gates were by then locked, she would return first thing in the morning. "Then before I shut the door, I pulled through the string of the latch, so that it could only be opened on the inside. I then shut it with some degree of force, that I might be sure of its being well shut. I said to the servant as I passed by (who was ignorant of the whole transaction) that he need not carry in candles yet as my Lord wanted to finish his prayers first."

From London, Lord Nithsdale made his way to Rome, where his wife eventually joined him. In Rome they happily spent the rest of their lives together.

The Tower of London from which Lord Nithsdale escaped in 1716 was greatly altered in appearance since it had been saved from destruction in the Great Fire of 1666. Fine new red brick armories between the Salt and Broad Arrow towers, and a great storehouse east of the Chapel of St. Peter ad Vincula had been built. Begun in the reign of James II, these splendid buildings had been finished in the time of William and Mary. In 1694, under the direction of Sir Christopher Wren, Surveyor General of His Majesty's Works, both the Bloody and Beauchamp towers had been "put in better repair than they [had] been in many years, being whited, moulded and made strong." And in later years Wren had been authorized to replace the Norman slits of the White Tower with the wider windows we see today, to provide new cupolas for its four turrets, and to carry out extensive repairs and alterations in brick to various towers in the inner curtain wall including a new doorway to the Martin Tower. All this new work, together with a large hospital block built to the north of the armories a few years after Wren's death in 1723, came near to destruction when a fierce fire erupted in the Tower on the night of October 30, 1841.

The fire broke out at half past ten in the Bowyer Tower, where a flue had become overheated. A sentinel who saw smoke issuing from a window at first took no action, but becoming alarmed as the clouds of smoke became more dense, he fired his musket. Soon the whole garrison had turned out, drums were beating the alarm, and the civilian inhabitants were pouring out onto Tower Green — "many in a state almost of nudity." The Tower's nine fire engines were trundled out of their sheds, but water could be found to supply only one of them. Engines that came from outside the walls to help were refused admittance by the guards at the gate, who interpreted very strictly their orders to let no one in.

By eleven o'clock the fire had almost completely destroyed the Bowyer Tower, and the flames had spread to the great armories and to the storehouse to the east of the Chapel of St. Peter ad Vincula — "a magnificent and stupendous structure" said *The Times* — which contained some splendid carvings by Grinling Gibbons.

At midnight the armories were burning fiercely, the apertures of the windows appearing to one observer like the craters of an erupting volcano. While thousands of people gathered on Tower Hill to watch the holocaust, and hundreds more — friends or relations of the inhabitants of the Tower — fought with police to gain entrance at the gates, the fire continued to spread. More fire engines had been brought into action now, but they seemed quite incapable of controlling the blaze, which by half past twelve in the morning threatened to devour the whole fortress. So intense was the heat from the burning armories and storehouse that the leaden water pipes on the walls of the White Tower melted, and the window frames began to smoulder and then burst into flames. The Brick Tower then caught fire and was soon burning as fiercely as the Bowyer Tower. Next the flames began to threaten the Martin Tower, where the crown jewels were stored.

Orders were now given that maximum efforts be made to save the regalia while there was still time; all the pieces were to be brought out and taken to the governor's house. A squad of soldiers was summoned to stand guard while this dangerous operation was being performed; but by the time the troops were in position, it was discovered that the Keeper of the Jewel House had only the key to the outer room. The other keys were in the possession of the Lord Chamberlain. It was then decided that the bars behind which the regalia lay would have to be bent back with crowbars, and the items lifted out piece by piece through the widened spaces. By the time the iron bars had been bent back, however, the heat was so intense that the guard was forced back from the door, and it was feared that the jewels would have to be abandoned to the flames.

At this point a brave police officer, encouraged by the Keeper of the Jewel House, determined to save what he could. While water was played upon the walls of the building by a group of firemen — one of whom was killed by a falling coping stone — the policeman handed out piece after piece through the bars, enduring a heat so intense that the cloth of his uniform was charred. Urged repeatedly to come out before it was too late, he remained in the Martin Tower until all the regalia, with the exception of a silver font that was too big to squeeze through the space between the bars, had been rescued.

At a quarter past three in the morning the fire was brought under control at last. By then, however, the armories and storehouse, the Bowyer Tower and the Brick Tower had all been completely destroyed, and both the White Tower and the Chapel of St. Peter ad Vincula had been badly damaged.

The Constable of the Tower at the time was the Duke of Wellington, who saw in the damage that had been done an opportunity to carry out extensive repairs to the whole structure of the Tower as well as to replace the buildings that had been burned down. So, backed by Prince Albert, Wellington persuaded the government to authorize an ambitious program of restoration and rebuilding that was continued throughout the rest of the nineteenth century.

The stagnant moat was drained, filled in with rubble, paved, and turned into a parade ground for the garrison; extensive repairs were made to the outer walls; the great architect Anthony Salvin was called in to rebuild the Salt Tower and the Bowyer Tower and to design a huge new barracks on the site of the destroyed storehouse. This was completed in 1845 and named the Waterloo Barracks. After Salvin's retirement, Sir John Taylor and J. R. Westcott continued working, and by the end of the century, the Cradle, Well, Broad Arrow, and Lanthorn towers had all been renovated; parts of the White Tower, the Chapel of St. Peter ad Vincula, and the upper half of the Bloody Tower had all been rebuilt.

Just as it had been feared in 1841 that the work of Wren and his predecessors would be totally destroyed by fire, so one Saturday afternoon in 1885 it was for a moment thought that all the subsequent work had been done in vain. At about two o'clock that day, January 24, there were, almost simultaneously, violent explosions in the Houses of Parliament, Westminster Hall, and the Tower of London. For months past there had been a series of bomb outrages all over the country

Doffing his Tudor bonnet, the Chief Yeoman Warder of the Tower utters his traditional cry, "God preserve Queen Elizabeth." That ancient phrase concludes a daily ritual known as the Ceremony of the Keys, symbolic of the Tower of London's nine-century-long association with the British monarchy and English history.

in what *The Times* referred to as "the Dynamite War." Those responsible were the Fenians, "disloyal Irish and the Irish-American outrage-mongers."

The "outrage-mongers" had planted their bomb in the former banqueting room of the White Tower at a time when it was full of visitors. The deafening explosion blew out the windows, tore an immense hole in the floor, and started a raging fire that threatened to spread fast to other buildings. While the visitors in the White Tower — several of whom were seriously injured — screamed in the billowing smoke, the garrison was called out by bugle and the Tower's fire brigade came into action.

Fortunately this fire brigade was far more efficient than the incompetent force that had struggled with the fire of 1841; the flames were soon brought under control, and the danger was overcome. Next day, the *Morning Post* reported that the Tower had been "saved to the inestimable benefit of a grateful nation that looked with pride upon the achievements of its past. It is to be hoped that this outrage will not deter visitors from enjoying the pleasures and lessons that the Tower has to offer to us all."

The explosion of 1885 did not deter visitors of that day, and the Tower remains, nearly a century later, one of the great wonders of Europe. No one who walks over the "Royal Palace and Fortress of London" — still the official name of the Tower of London — can fail to be moved by the stories of those men and women who have lived and been happy, have languished in misery, have died a violent death within its walls during the course of nine hundred years. Nor can anyone witness the ancient Ceremony of the Keys, which takes place every night at ten o'clock, and fail to respond to the echoes of the past.

The Chief Yeoman Warder, in long red cloak and Tudor bonnet, carrying a lantern in which there burns a tallow candle, marches out toward the Byward Tower with the keys of the fortress in his hand. He calls out: "An escort for the Keys." Four armed soldiers of the garrison fall into step beside him, and they march with him through the gates of the Byward Tower and over the causeway to the entrance gate beyond the Middle Tower. The gate is locked; the escort marches back in the darkness toward the towers of the outer ward; there is a clanking of metal as the gates of the Byward Tower are locked and the bolts shot home. As the Chief Yeoman Warder and his escort approach the Bloody Tower, the sentry on guard comes forward with the challenge:

"Halt, who goes there?"

The Chief Yeoman Warder replies, as his predecessors have replied every night for centuries, "The Keys."

"Whose Keys?"

"Queen Elizabeth's keys."

The sentry presents arms, the Chief Yeoman Warder doffs his bonnet and calls out, "God preserve Queen Elizabeth!"

The whole guard responds, "Amen!"

The escort moves on through the archway of the Bloody Tower, the light of the lantern shining on the old gray stone. Another day in the crowded history of the Tower of London is ended.

THE
TOWER OF LONDON
IN LITERATURE

Reproduced above and on the following pages are a number of seventeenth-century playing cards depicting events at the Tower during the Popish Plot and the Monmouth and Essex rebellions.

LADIES IMPRISONED

In 1536 the most famous of Henry VIII's six wives awaited execution in the Queen's House at the Tower. Charged with committing incest and adultery, Anne Boleyn's real offense was her apparent inability to provide Henry with a male heir. In order to marry Anne, Henry had broken with Pope Clement VII, who had refused to grant him a divorce from his first wife. The breach with Rome led to the establishment of a separate Church of England and the subsequent executions of such notables as Sir Thomas More, John Fisher, and John Houghton, all of whom refused to recognize Henry as the spiritual head of the new church. Anne felt responsible for their deaths. Time would grant her deepest wish, however: her daughter Elizabeth would eventually rule England. The tragic love story of Henry and Anne was the inspiration of Maxwell Anderson's Anne of the Thousand Days, *one of his most moving works. Anne is the speaker; the time is May 18, 1536, the evening before her execution.*

If I were to die now —
but I must not die yet,
not yet.
It's been too brief. A few weeks and days.
How many days, I wonder, since the first time
I gave myself, to that last day when he —
when he left me at the lists and I saw him no more?
Well, I can reckon it.
I have time enough. Those who sit in the Tower
don't lack for time.
(*She takes out a little wax tablet, with a stylus*)
He could never cipher.
He was shrewd and heavy —
and cunning with his tongue, and wary in intrigue,
but when it came to adding up an account
he filled it with errors and bit his tongue —
and swore —
till I slapped his hands like a child and took the pen
and made it straight.
"A king," I said, "a king, and cannot reckon."
I was his clever girl then, his Nan;
he'd kiss me then, and maul me, and take me down.
On the rushes. Anywhere.
Why do I think of it now? Would he kill me? Kill me?
(*She laughs*)
Henry? The fool? That great fool kill me?
God knows I deserve it. God knows I tried to kill,
and it may be I succeeded.
I did succeed. I know too well I succeeded,
and I'm guilty, for I brought men to death unjustly,
as this death of mine will be unjust if it comes —
only I taught them the way. And I'm to die
in the way I contrived. . . . It may be. . . .
No, but Henry. He could not. Could not. . .
Could I kill him, I wonder?
I feel it in my hands perhaps I could.

So — perhaps he could kill me.
Perhaps he could kill me.
If it came tomorrow, how many days
would it have been,
(She makes a mark on the tablet)
beginning with our first day? . . .
From the day he first made me his,
to the last day I made him mine,
yes,
let me set it down in numbers,
I who can count and reckon, and have the time.
Of all the days I was his and did not love him —
this; and this; and this many.
Of all the days I was his —
and he had ceased to love me —
this many; and this. In days.
(She writes)
It comes to a thousand days —
out of the years.
Strangely, just a thousand.
And of that thousand —
one —
when we were both in love. Only one
when our loves met, and overlapped and were both mine and his.
When I no longer hated him —
he began to hate me,
except for that day. And the son we had —
the one son — born of our hate and lust —
died in my womb. When Henry was hurt at the jousting.
Then Henry looked in my face and said,
"This marriage is cursed like the other.
I've known it all along.
There's a curse on it."
And he turned and left me.
Have you no hate in your heart, Anne?
You had hate enough when you were young!
Hate him now, and curse him, and it won't matter
what he does — or has done! I can't hate him.
It's as he said long ago:
You love where you love.
You can't change it. And this great fool and bully,
I'd take him now
if he came and put out his hand
and said one word.
(The lights dim, remaining on Anne's face, then coming up on stage left)
Even when they came. . . .
. . . I've never thought what it was like to die.
To become meat that rots. Then food for shrubs,
and the long roots of vines.
The grape could reach me.
I may make him drunk before many years.

A Papist in disguise
taken at $\tilde{y}$ Tower.

Someone told me the story
of the homely daughter of Sir Thomas More
climbing at night up the trestles of London Bridge
where they'd stuck her father's head on a spike —
and climbing down with it, and taking it home.
To bury in the garden perhaps.
Even so, it was death. And I ordered it.
And Bishop Fisher, the old frail man.
And Houghton.
And the thousands.
They lie there now. And the roots find them.
— That was my dream! I remember —
poor homely Margaret
climbing into the darkness above the bridge
and hunting among the stinking and bloody heads
of criminals, till she found her father's head,
and pulling it from the spike,
holding on with one hand, crying, almost falling,
his beard matted and hard with blood.
Then she must clasp the horrible thing against her breast,
and climb down in the dark, holding by one hand,
slipping, near falling, unable to see for tears.
"Where is your father's head?" they asked her.
"In earth," she said proudly. "How far do you pursue
    a great man after his death?"
And they haven't found it, still. . . .
Would they fix my head up on London Bridge?
No. Even Henry would object to that.
I've been his queen. He's kissed my lips.
He wouldn't want it. I'll lie in lead — or brass. Meat. Dead meat.
But if my head were on the bridge he wouldn't climb to take it down.
Nobody'd climb for me. I could stay and face up the river,
and my long hair blow out and tangle round
the spikes — and my small neck.
Till the sea birds took me,
and there was nothing but a wisp of hair
and a cup of bone.
Sir Thomas More made a jest before he died.
He spoke to the headsman at the foot of the scaffold —
"Friend," he said, "if you'll help me to get up,
I'll see to the coming down."
I must think of something to say when the time comes.
If I could say it — with the ax edge toward me.
Could I do it? Could I lay my head down —
and smile, and speak? Till the blow comes?
They say it's subtle. It doesn't hurt. There's no time.
No time. That's the end of time.
I wonder what will come of my little girl
when she must go on alone.

MAXWELL ANDERSON
Anne of the Thousand Days, 1948

Alfred Lord Tennyson, poet laureate and a commanding literary figure of the Victorian Age, set his historical drama Queen Mary *in and around the Tower. In this memorable and climactic scene, only moments before she learns of the death of her half sister, Queen Mary, the twenty-five-year-old Princess Elizabeth, daughter of Henry VIII by Anne Boleyn, recalls the horror of her imprisonment at the Bell Tower.*

I would I were a milkmaid,
To sing, love, marry, churn, brew, bake, and die,
Then have my simple headstone by the church,
And all things lived and ended honestly.
I could not if I would. I am Harry's daughter. . . .
I never lay my head upon the pillow
But that I think, "Wilt thou lie there to-morrow?"
How oft the falling axe, that never fell,
Hath shock'd me back into the daylight truth
That it may fall to-day! Those damp, black, dead
Nights in the Tower; dead — with the fear of death —
Too dead ev'n for a death-watch! Toll of a bell,
Stroke of a clock, the scurrying of a rat
Affrighted me, and then delighted me,
For there was life — And there was life in death —
The little murder'd princes, in a pale light,
Rose hand in hand, and whisper'd, "come away,
The civil wars are gone forevermore:
Thou last of all the Tudors, come away,
With us is peace!" The last? It was a dream;
I must not dream, not wink, but watch.

ALFRED LORD TENNYSON
Queen Mary: A Drama, 1875

Lord Nithsdale, imprisoned at the Tower in 1715 for leading an uprising in support of a Scottish pretender to the English throne, escaped certain death at the eleventh hour through the boldness and ingenuity of his wife. History is fortunate in having a firsthand account of the escapade, a letter from Lady Nithsdale written only three years later.

Dear Sister. . . . I first came to London upon hearing that my Lord was committed to the Tower. I was at the same time informed, that he had expressed the greatest anxiety to see me; having, as he afterwards told me, nobody to console him till I arrived. . . .

On my arrival, I went immediately to make what interest I could among those who were in place. No one gave me any hopes; but all, to the contrary, assured me, that although some of the prisoners were to be pardoned, yet my Lord would certainly not be of the number. . . .

Upon this I formed the resolution to attempt his escape, but opened my intentions to nobody but to my dear Evans. In order to concert measures, I strongly solicited to be permitted to see my Lord, which they refused to grant me unless I would remain confined with him in the Tower. This I would not submit to, and alleged for an excuse, that my health would not permit me to undergo the confinement. The real reason of my refusal was, not to put it out of my power to accomplish my design; however, by bribing the guards, I often contrived to see my Lord, till the day upon which the prisoners were condemned; after that we were allowed for the last week to see and take our leave of them.

By the help of Evans, I had prepared everything necessary to disguise my Lord, but had the utmost difficulty to prevail upon him to make use of them; however, I at length succeeded by the help of Almighty God. . . .

The next morning I could not go to the Tower, having so many things in my hands to put in readiness; but in the evening, when all was ready, I went for Mrs. Mills, with whom I lodged, and acquainted her with my design of attempting my Lord's escape, as there was no prospect of his being pardoned; and this was the last night before the execution. I told her that I had everything in readiness, and that I trusted she would not refuse to accompany me, that my Lord might pass for her. I pressed her to come immediately, as we had no time to lose. At the same time I sent for Mrs. Morgan, then usually known by the name of Hilton, to whose acquaintance my dear Evans has introduced me, which I looked upon as a very singular happiness. I immediately communicated my resolution to her. She was of a very tall and slender make; so I begged her to put under her own riding-hood one that I had prepared for Mrs. Mills, as she was to lend hers to my Lord, that, in coming out, he might be taken for her. Mrs. Mills was then with child; so that she was not only of the same height, but nearly the same size as my Lord. When we were in the coach, I never ceased talking, that they might have no leisure to reflect. Their surprise and astonishment when I first opened my design to them, had made them consent, without ever thinking of the consequences. On our arrival at the Tower, the first I introduced was Mrs. Morgan; for I was only allowed to take in one at a time. She brought in the clothes that were to serve Mrs. Mills, when she left her own behind her. When Mrs. Morgan had taken off what she had brought for my purpose, I conducted her back to the staircase, and, in going, I begged her to send me in my maid to dress me; that I was afraid of being too late to present my last petition that night, if she did not come immediately. I despatched her safe, and went partly down stairs to meet Mrs. Mills, who had the precaution to hold her handkerchief to her face, as was very natural for a woman to do when she was going to bid her last farewell to a friend on the eve of his execution. I had, indeed, desired her to do it, that my Lord might go out in the same manner. Her eyebrows were rather inclined to be sandy, and my Lord's were dark and very thick: however, I had prepared some paint of the colour of hers to disguise his with. I also bought an artificial head-dress of the same coloured hair as hers; and I painted his face with white and his cheeks with rouge, to hide his long beard, which he had not had time to shave. All this provision I had before left in the Tower. The poor guards, whom my slight liberality the day before had endeared me to, let me go quietly with my company, and were not so strictly on the watch as they usually had been; and the more so, as they were persuaded, from what I had told them the day before, that the prisoners would obtain their pardon. I made Mrs. Mills take off her own hood, and put on that which I had brought for her. I then took her by the hand, and led her out of my Lord's chamber; and, in passing through the next room, in which there were several people, with all the concern imaginable, I said, "My dear Mrs. Catherine, go in all haste, and send me my wait-

Severall disaffected Lds sent to ye Tower

ing-maid: she certainly cannot reflect how late it is: she forgets that I am to present a petition to-night; and if I let slip this opportunity, I am undone; for to-morrow will be too late. Hasten her as much as possible; for I shall be on thorns till she comes." Everybody in the room, who were chiefly the guards' wives and daughters, seemed to compassionate me exceedingly; and the sentinel officiously opened the door. When I had seen her out, I returned back to my Lord, and finished dressing him. I had taken care that Mrs. Mills did not go out crying as she came in, that my Lord might the better pass for the lady who came in crying and afflicted; and the more so because he had the same dress she wore. When I had almost finished dressing my Lord in all my petticoats, excepting one, I perceived that it was growing dark, and was afraid that the light of the candles might betray us; so I resolved to set off. I went out, leading him by the hand; and he held his handkerchief to his eyes. I spoke to him in the most piteous and afflicted tone of voice, bewailing bitterly the negligence of Evans, who had ruined me by her delay. Then said I, "My dear Mrs. Betty, for the love of God, run quickly and bring her with you. You know my lodgings; and, if ever you made despatch in your life, do it at present: I am almost distracted with this disappointment." The guards opened the doors, and I went down stairs with him, still conjuring him to make all possible despatch. As soon as he had cleared the door, I made him walk before me, for fear the sentinel should take notice of his walk; but I still continued to press him to make all the despatch he possibly could. At the bottom of the stairs I met my dear Evans, into whose hands I confided him. . . .

In the meanwhile, as I had pretended to have sent the young lady on a message, I was obliged to return up stairs, and go back to my Lord's room, in the same feigned anxiety of being too late; so that every body seemed sincerely to sympathise with my distress. When I was in the room, I talked to him as if he had been really present, and answered my own questions in my Lord's voice as nearly as I could imitate it. I walked up and down, as if we were conversing together, till I thought they had time enough thoroughly to clear themselves of the guards. I then thought proper to make off also. I opened the door, and stood half in it, that those in the outward chamber might hear what I said; but held it so close that they could not look in. I bid my Lord a formal farewell for that night, and added, that something more than usual must have happened to make Evans negligent on this important occasion, who had always been so punctual in the smallest trifles; that I saw no other remedy than to go in person; that, if the Tower were still open when I finished my business, I would return that night; but that he might be assured I would be with him as early in the morning as I could gain admittance into the Tower; and I flattered myself I should bring favourable news. Then, before I shut the door, I pulled through the string of the latch, so that it could only be opened on the inside. I then shut it with some degree of force, that I might be sure of its being well shut. I said to the servant as I passed by, who was ignorant of the whole transaction, that he need not carry in candles to his master till my Lord sent for him, as he desired to finish some prayers first. I went down stairs and called a coach. . . .

. . . [Evans] had removed my Lord . . . to the house of a poor woman directly opposite to the guard-house. She had but one small room, up one pair of stairs, and a very small bed in it. We threw ourselves upon the bed, that we might not be heard walking up and down. She left us a bottle of wine and some bread, and Mrs. Mills brought us some more in her pocket the next day. We subsisted on this provision from Thursday till Saturday night, when Mrs. Mills came and conducted my Lord to the Venetian Ambassador's. We did not communicate the affair to his Excellency; but one of his servants concealed him in his own room till Wednesday, on which day the Ambassador's coach and six was to go down to Dover to meet his brother. My Lord put on a livery, and went down in the retinue, without the least suspicion, to Dover, where Mr. Mitchell (which was the name of the Ambassador's servant) hired a small vessel and immediately set sail for Calais. The passage was so remarkably short, that the captain threw out this reflection, that the wind could not have served better if his passengers had been flying for their lives, little thinking it to be really the case. . . .

This is as exact and as full an account of this affair, and of the persons concerned in it, as I could possibly give you, to the best of my memory, and you may rely on the truth of it. I am, with the strongest attachment, my dear Sister, yours, most affectionately,

WINIFRED NITHSDALE
Letter to Her Sister, 1718

SHAKESPEARE'S LITTLE PRINCES

In his Richard III, *Shakespeare portrayed the future king as a ruthless opportunist. To gain the throne, Richard, Duke of Gloucester, first had to eliminate those in line for the succession: the Duke of Clarence and his young nephews, the Prince of Wales and the Duke of York. With Buckingham's help, Richard persuades the princes to enter the Tower, knowing they will never leave it alive. Although Shakespeare states that Julius Caesar built the Tower, there is no evidence for this tradition.*

PRINCE. . . . Where shall we sojourn till our coronation?
GLOUCESTER [RICHARD III]   Where it seems best unto your royal self.
If I may counsel you, some day or two
Your Highness shall repose you at the Tower:
Then where you please, and shall be thought most fit
For your best health and recreation.
PRINCE   I do not like the Tower, of any place:
Did Julius Caesar build that place, my lord?
BUCKINGHAM   He did, my gracious lord, begin that place,
Which, since, succeeding ages have re-edified.
PRINCE   Is it upon record, or else reported
Successively from age to age, he built it?
BUCKINGHAM   Upon record, my gracious lord.
PRINCE   But say, my lord, it were not register'd,
Methinks the truth shall live from age to age,
As 'twere retail'd to all posterity,
Even to the general all-ending day.
GLOUCESTER (*Aside*)   So wise so young, they say, do never live long.
PRINCE   What say you, uncle?
GLOUCESTER   I say, without characters, fame lives long.
(*Aside*) Thus, like the formal Vice, Iniquity,
I moralize two meanings in one word.
PRINCE   That Julius Caesar was a famous man;
With what his valour did enrich his wit,

His wit set down to make his valour live:
Death makes no conquest of this conqueror,
For now he lives in fame, though not in life.
I'll tell you what, my cousin Buckingham, —
BUCKINGHAM   What, my gracious lord?
PRINCE   An if I live until I be a man,
I'll win our ancient right in France again,
Or die a soldier, as I liv'd a king.
GLOUCESTER (*Aside*)   Short summers lightly have a forward spring. . . .
GLOUCESTER   My lord, will't please you pass along?
Myself and my good cousin Buckingham
Will to your mother, to entreat of her
To meet you at the Tower and welcome you.
YORK   What! will you go unto the Tower, my lord?
PRINCE   My Lord Protector needs will have it so.
YORK   I shall not sleep in quiet at the Tower.
GLOUCESTER   Why, what would you fear?
YORK   Marry, my uncle Clarence' angry ghost:
My grandam told me he was murder'd there.
PRINCE   I fear no uncles dead.
GLOUCESTER   Nor none that live, I hope.
PRINCE   An if they live, I hope, I need not fear.
But come, my lord; and, with a heavy heart,
Thinking on them, go I unto the Tower. . . .

> *Following their imprisonment, the princes are murdered, and the villain
> hired by Richard to kill them expresses a belated sense of conscience in
> a soliloquy.*

TYRRELL   The tyrannous and bloody act is done;
The most arch deed of piteous massacre
That ever yet this land was guilty of.
Dighton and Forrest, whom I did suborn
To do this piece of ruthless butchery,
Albeit they were flesh'd villains, bloody dogs,
Melting with tenderness and mild compassion,
Wept like to children in their death's sad story.
'Oh! thus,' quoth Dighton, 'lay the gentle babes':
'Thus, thus,' quoth Forrest, 'girdling one another
Within their alabaster innocent arms:
Their lips were four red roses on a stalk,
Which in their summer beauty kiss'd each other.
A book of prayers on their pillow lay;
Which once,' quoth Forrest, 'almost chang'd my mind;
But, O, the devil' — there the villain stopp'd;
When Dighton thus told on: 'We smothered
The most replenished sweet work of nature,
That from the prime creation e'er she fram'd.'
Hence both are gone with conscience and remorse;
They could not speak; and so I left them both,
To bear this tidings to the bloody king.

WILLIAM SHAKESPEARE
Richard the Third, c. 1594

GHOST STORIES

To the superstitious historian Matthew Paris, the disgruntled ghost of Thomas à Becket was responsible for a series of mysterious disasters at St. Thomas's Tower in the thirteenth century.

About this time [1241] a vision appeared by night to a certain priest, a wise and holy man, wherein an archprelate, dressed in pontifical robes, and carrying a cross in his hand, came to the walls which the king had at that time built near the Tower of London, and, after regarding them with a scowling look, struck them strongly and violently with the cross, saying, "Why do ye rebuild them?" Whereupon the newly-erected walls suddenly fell to the ground, as if thrown down by an earthquake. The priest, frightened at this sight, said to a clerk who appeared following the archprelate, "Who is this archbishop?" to which the clerk replied, "It is St. Thomas the martyr, a Londoner by birth, who considered that these walls were built as an insult, and to the prejudice of the Londoners, and has therefore irreparably destroyed them." The priest then said, "What expense and builders' labour have they not cost." The clerk replied, "If poor artificers, who seek after and have need of pay, had obtained food for themselves by the work, that would be endurable; but inasmuch as they have been built, not for the defence of the kingdom, but only to oppress harmless citizens, if St. Thomas had not destroyed them, St. Edmund the confessor and his successor would still more relentlessly have overthrown them from their foundations." The priest, after having seen these things, awoke from his sleep, rose from his bed, and, in the dead silence of the night, told his vision to all who were in the house. Early in the morning a report spread through the city of London that the walls built round the Tower, on the construction of which the king had expended more than twelve thousand marks, had fallen to pieces, to the wonder of many, who proclaimed it a bad omen, because the year before, on the same night, which was that of St. George's day, and at the same hour of the night, the said walls had fallen down, together with their bastions. The citizens of London, although astonished at this event, were not sorry for it; for these walls were to them as a thorn in their eyes, and they had heard the taunts of people who said that these walls had been built as an insult to them, and that if any one of them should dare to contend for the liberty of the city, he would be shut up in them, and consigned to imprisonment; and in order that, if several were to be imprisoned, they might be confined in several different prisons, a great number of cells were constructed in them apart from one another, that one person might not have communication with another.

MATTHEW PARIS
English History, c. 1259

In a 1913 article in England's Occult Review, *Elliott O'Donnell cited the eerie experience of the Keeper of the Crown Jewels as the "best authenticated haunting" in the Tower's history.*

I have often purposed to leave behind me a faithful record of all that I personally know of this strange story. . . . Forty-three years have passed, and its impression is as vividly before me as at the moment of its occurrence . . . but there are yet survivors who can testify that I have not at any time either amplified or abridged my ghostly experiences.

In 1814 I was appointed Keeper of the Crown Jewels in the Tower, where I resided with my family till my retirement in 1852. One Saturday night in October, 1817, about the witching hour, I was at supper with my wife, her sister, and our little boy, in the sitting-room of the Jewel House, which — then completely modernized — is said to have been the doleful prison of Anne Boleyn, and of the ten bishops whom Oliver Cromwell piously accommodated therein.

The room was — as it still is — irregularly shaped, having three doors and two windows, which last are cut nearly nine feet deep into the outer wall; between those is a chimneypiece, projecting far into the room, and (then) surmounted with a large oil-painting. On the night in question the doors were all closed, heavy and dark cloth curtains were let down over the windows, and the only light in the room was that of two candles on the table. I sate at the foot of the table, my son on my right hand, his mother fronting the chimneypiece, and her sister on the opposite side. I had offered a glass of wine and water to my wife, when, on putting it to her lips, she paused and exclaimed, "Good God! What is that?"

I looked up, and saw a cylindrical figure, like a glass tube, seemingly about the thickness of my arm, and hovering between the ceiling and the table; its contents appeared to be a dense fluid, white and pale azure, like to the gathering of a summer cloud, and incessantly mingling within the cylinder. This lasted about two minutes, when it began slowly to move before my sister-in-law; then following the oblong shape of the table, before my son and myself, passing behind my wife, it paused for a moment over her right shoulder; instantly she crouched down, and with both hands covering her shoulder, she shrieked out, "Oh, Christ, it has seized me!" Even now, while writing, I feel the fresh horror of that moment.

I caught up the chair, struck at the wainscot behind her, rushed upstairs to the other children's rooms, and told the terrified nurse what I had seen. Meanwhile, the other domestics had hurried into the parlour where the mistress recounted to them the scene, even as I was detailing it above stairs. The marvel of all this is enhanced by the fact that neither my sister-in-law nor my son beheld this appearance. When I, the next morning, related the night's horror to our chaplain, after the service in the Tower Church, he asked me, might not one person have his natural senses deceived? And if one, why not two? My answer was, if two, why not two thousand? An argument which would reduce history, secular or sacred, to a fable.

EDMUND LENTHAL SWIFTE
1860

The late D: of M: L.ᵈ Grey & a German carried to yᵉ Tower

Also from O'Donnell's article comes this tale of an aged guard's encounter with the lovesick ghost of King Henry VIII.

Is the Tower of London haunted? . . . why of course it is! Haunted by all sorts of ghosts — legions of them. I remember one of them particularly well. It was when I was on dooty in the Beauchamp Tower, just outside the cell where Anne Boleyn was imprisoned. I was thinking of old Henry VIII, and wishing I had his luck with wives, for my one and only old missis was as ugly as Newgate, when all of a sudden I heard my name called, and on turning round, nearly died with fright. Floating in mid-air, immediately behind me, was a face — God help me, it makes me shiver, even now, to think of it — round, red and bloated, with a loose, dribbling mouth, and protruding, heavy-lidded, pale eyes, alight with a lurid and perfectly 'ellish glow.

I knew the face at once, for I had often seen it in the history books — 'Enery VIII. 'Enery with all the devil showing in him. I was so scared that I ran, and did not stop running, till I came upon two of my comrades, who were beginning to clamour out "What's the matter?" when they suddenly broke off — the face had followed me.

Well! to cut a long story short, the affair was hushed up and in the usual way. We were all threatened with the sack if we dare as much as breathe a word that the Tower was 'aunted. The oddest thing about it, 'owever, is, that on my return home, I found my missus was dead. She had died the very moment I saw the 'ead. I suppose old 'Arry wanted her. Well, as far as I am concerned he's 'ighly welcome to her. At all events he'll never get rid of her. She'll stick to him like porous plaster.

ANONYMOUS
c. 1890

THE GREAT FIRE

The famed diarist Samuel Pepys left a charming record of seventeenth-century London society. Pepys often visited the Tower, where he dined with its officials or watched executions. In 1666, according to his own account, he was instrumental in saving the monument from destruction.

[September 2, 1666]

Some of our maids sitting up late last night to get things ready against our feast to-day, Jane called us up about three in the morning, to tell us of a great fire they saw in the City. So I rose, and slipped on my nightgown, and went to her window; and thought it to be on the back-side of Marke-lane at the farthest; but, being unused to such fires as followed, I thought it far enough off; and so went to bed again, and to sleep. About seven rose again to dress myself, and there looked out at the window, and saw the fire not so much as it was, and further off. . . . By and by Jane [the maid] comes and tells me that she hears that above 300 houses have been burned down to-night by the fire we saw, and that it is now burning down all Fish Street, by London Bridge. So I made myself ready presently, and walked to the Tower; and there got up upon one of the high places, Sir J. Robinson's little son going up with me; and there did I see the houses at that end of the bridge all on fire, and an infinite great fire on this and the other side of the bridge; which, among other people, did trouble me for little Michell and our Sarah on the bridge. So down, with my heart full of trouble, to the Lieutenant of the Tower, who tells me that it begun this morning in the King's baker's house in Pudding-lane, and that it hath burned down St. Magnus's Church and most part of Fish Street already. So I down to the water-side, and there got a boat, and through bridge, and there saw a lamentable fire. Poor Michell's house, as far as the Old Swan, already burned that way, and the fire running further, that, in a very little time, it got as far as the Steeleyard, while I was there. Every body endeavouring to remove their goods, and flinging into the river, or bringing them into lighters that lay off; poor people staying in their houses as long as till the very fire touched them, and then running into boats, or clambering from one pair of stairs, by the waterside, to another. And, among other things, the poor pigeons, I perceive, were loth to leave their houses, but hovered about the windows and balconys, till they burned their wings, and fell down. Having staid, and in an hour's time seen the fire rage every way; and nobody, to my sight, endeavouring to quench it, but to remove their goods, and leave all to the fire; and, having seen it get as far as the Steele-yard, and the wind mighty high, and driving it into the City; and everything, after so long a drought, proving combustible, even the very stones of churches; and, among other things, the poor steeple by which pretty Mrs. ——— lives, and whereof my old schoolfellow Elborough is parson, taken fire in the very top, and there burned till it fell down; I to White Hall, with a gentleman with me, who desired to go off from the Tower, to see the fire, in my boat; and there up to the King's closet in the Chapel, where people come about me, and I did give them an account dismayed them all, and word was carried in to the King. So I was called for, and did tell the King and Duke of York what I saw; and that, unless his Majesty did command houses to be pulled down, nothing could stop the fire. They seemed much troubled, and the King commanded me to go to my Lord Mayor from him, and command him to spare no houses, but to pull [them] down. . . .

[September 3]

About four o'clock in the morning, my Lady Batten sent me a cart to carry away all my money, and plate, and best things, to Sir W. Rider's, at Bednall Greene, which I did, riding myself in my night-gown, in the cart; and, Lord! to see how the streets and the highways are crowded with people running and riding, and getting of carts at any rate to fetch away things. I find Sir W. Rider tired with being called up all night, and receiving things from several friends. His house full of goods, and much of Sir W. Batten's and Sir W. Pen's. I am eased at my heart to have my treasure so well secured. Then home, and with much ado to find a way, nor any sleep all this night to me nor my poor wife. But then all this day she and I and all my people labouring to get away the rest of our things, and did get Mr. Tooker to get me a lighter to take them in, and we did carry them, myself some, over Tower Hill, which was by this time full of people's goods, bringing their goods thither; and down to the lighter, which lay at the next quay, above the Tower Dock. . . .

[September 4]

Up by break of day, to get away the remainder of my things; which I did by a lighter at the Iron gate: and my hands so full, that it was the afternoon before we could get them all away. Sir W. Pen and I to the Tower Street, and there met the fire burning, three or four doors beyond Mr. Howell's, whose goods, poor man, his trayes, and dishes, shovells, &c., were flung all along Tower Street in the kennels, and people working therewith from one end to the other; the fire coming on in that narrow street, on both sides, with infinite fury. . . . I after supper walked in the dark down to Tower Street, and there saw it all on fire, at the Trinity House on that side, and the Dolphin Tavern on this side, which was very near us; and the fire with extraordinary vehemence. Now begins the practice of blowing up of houses in Tower Street, those next the Tower, which at first did frighten people more than any thing; but it stopped the fire where it was done, it bringing down the houses to the ground in the same places they stood, and then it was easy to quench what little fire was in it, though it kindled nothing almost.

SAMUEL PEPYS

Diary and Correspondence, 1666

The Chancellor going to the Tower and is followed by many more of Brethren.

"MEN MAY BLEED AND MEN MAY BURN"

Sir Walter Scott's longest novel, Peveril of the Peak, *is set against the Popish Plot of 1678, which was not a plot at all, but a bloody reaction to rumors that Jesuits planned to overthrow the Protestant government and set up a Catholic one. The central figure of the book, which contains 108 characters, is Julian Peveril, a Catholic arrested during the scare and imprisoned at the Tower with his parents. Ultimately, all are acquitted, and Julian is reunited with his Protestant sweetheart, Alice Bridgenorth.*

The Tower! — it was a word of terror, even more so than a civil prison; for how many passages to death did that dark structure present! The severe executions which it had witnessed in preceding reigns, were not perhaps more numerous than the secret murders which had taken place within its walls; yet Peveril did not a moment hesitate on the part which he had to perform. "I will share my father's fate," he said; "I thought but of him when they brought me hither; I will think of nothing else when they convey me to yonder still more dreadful place of confinement; it is his, and it is but meet that it should be his son's. — And thou, Alice Bridgenorth, the day that I renounce thee may I be held alike a traitor and a dastard! . . ."

. . . the turnkey . . . opening the door with unusual precautions to avoid noise, had stolen unperceived into the room. . . .

"I am to be removed, then?" said Julian.

"Ay, truly, master, the warrant is come from the Council."

"To convey me to the Tower."

"Whew!" exclaimed the officer of the law — "who the devil told you that? But since you do know it, there is no harm to say ay. So make yourself ready to move immediately. . . ."

. . . Julian . . . was led along the same stern passages which he had traversed upon his entrance, to the gate of the prison, whence a coach, escorted by two officers of justice, conveyed him to the water-side. . . .

. . . [He] remained silent until the boat came under the dusky bastions of the Tower. The tide carried them up under a dark and lowering arch, closed at the upper end by the well-known Traitor's Gate, formed like a wicket of huge intersecting bars of wood, through which might be seen a dim and imperfect view of soldiers and warders upon duty, and of the steep ascending causeway which leads up from the river into the interior of the fortress. By this gate, — and it is the well-known circumstance which assigned its name, — those accused of state crimes were usually committed to the Tower. The Thames afforded a secret and silent mode of conveyance for transporting thither such whose fallen fortunes might move the commiseration, or whose popular qualities might excite the sympathy, of the public; and even where no cause for especial secrecy existed, the peace of the city was undisturbed by the tumult attending the passage of the prisoner and his guards through the most frequented streets.

Yet this custom, however recommended by state policy, must have often struck chill upon the heart of the criminal, who thus, stolen, as it were, out of society, reached the place of his confinement, without encountering even one glance of compassion on the road; and as, from under the dusky arch, he landed on those flinty steps, worn by many a footstep anxious as his own, against which the tide lapped fitfully with small successive waves, and thence looked forward to the steep ascent into a Gothic state-prison, and backward to such part of the river as the low-brow'd vault suffered to become visible, he must often have felt that he was leaving daylight, hope, and life itself, behind him.

While the warder's challenge was made and answered, Peveril endeavoured to obtain information from his conductors where he was likely to be confined; but the answer was brief and general — "Where the Lieutenant should direct."

"Could he not be permitted to share the imprisonment of his father, Sir Geoffrey Peveril?" He forgot not, on this occasion, to add the surname of his house.

The warder, an old man of respectable appearance, stared, as if at the extravagance of the demand, and said bluntly, "It is impossible."

"At least," said Peveril, "show me where my father is confined, that I may look upon the walls which separate us."

"Young gentleman," said the senior warder, shaking his gray head, "I am sorry for you; but asking questions will do you no service. In this place we know nothing of fathers and sons."

Yet chance seemed, in a few minutes afterwards, to offer Peveril that satisfaction which the rigour of his keepers was disposed to deny to him. As he was conveyed up the steep passage which leads under what is called the Wakefield Tower, a female voice, in a tone wherein grief and joy were indescribably mixed, exclaimed, "My son! — My dear son!"

The Seaven Biſshops going to the Tower.

Even those who guarded Julian seemed softened by a tone of such acute feeling. They slackened their pace. They almost paused to permit him to look up towards the casement from which the sounds of maternal agony proceeded; but the aperture was so narrow, and so closely grated, that nothing was visible save a white female hand, which grasped one of those rusty barricadoes, as if for supporting the person within, while another streamed a white handkerchief, and then let it fall. The casement was instantly deserted.

"Give it to me," said Julian to the officer who lifted the handkerchief; "it is perhaps a mother's last gift."

The old warder lifted the napkin, and looked at it with the jealous minuteness of one who is accustomed to detect secret correspondence in the most trifling acts of intercourse.

"There may be writing on it with invisible ink," said one of his comrades.

"It is wetted, but I think it is only with tears," answered the senior. "I cannot keep it from the poor young gentleman."

"Ah, Master Coleby," said his comrade, in a gentle tone of reproach, "you would have been wearing a better coat than a yeoman's to-day, had it not been for your tender heart."

"It signifies little," said old Coleby, "while my heart is true to my King, what I feel in discharging my duty, or what coat keeps my old bosom from the cold weather."

Peveril, meanwhile, folded in his breast the token of his mother's affection which chance had favoured him with; and when placed in the small and solitary chamber which he was told to consider as his own during his residence in the Tower, he was soothed even to weeping by this trifling circumstance, which he could not help considering as an omen, that his unfortunate house was not entirely deserted by Providence.

SIR WALTER SCOTT
Peveril of the Peak, 1823

In the late nineteenth century, the Tower became the setting for Gilbert and Sullivan's The Yeomen of the Guard. *The comic opera's whimsical plot includes the imprisonment of a dashing young colonel on charges of sorcery, a frenetic escape plan concocted by a sympathetic yeoman, assorted love triangles and, inevitably, a happy ending for all. In the first act, Dame Carruthers, the garrulous Housekeeper of the Tower, sings an ode that reveals her deep affection for the monument.*

DAME. . . . I was born in the old keep, and I've grown gray in it, and, please God, I shall die and be buried in it; and there's not a stone in its walls that is not as dear to me as my own right hand. . . .

When our gallant Norman foes
   Made our merry land their own,
      And the Saxons from the Conqueror were flying,
At his bidding it arose,
   In its panoply of stone,
      A sentinel unliving and undying.
Insensible, I trow,
   As a sentinel should be,
      Though a queen to save her head should come a-suing,
There's a legend on its brow
   That is eloquent to me,
      And it tells of duty done and duty doing.

The screw may twist and the rack may turn,
And men may bleed and men may burn,
On London town and all its hoard
I keep my solemn watch and ward!

CHORUS
The screw may twist, etc.

Within its wall of rock
   The flower of the brave
      Have perished with a constancy unshaken.
From the dungeon to the block,
   From the scaffold to the grave,
      Is a journey many gallant hearts have taken.

And the wicked flames may hiss
   Round the heroes who have fought
      For conscience and for home in all its beauty,
But the grim old fortalice
   Takes little heed of aught
      That comes not in the measure of its duty.

The screw may twist and the rack may turn,
And men may bleed and men may burn,
On London town and all its hoard
It keeps its silent watch and ward!

WILLIAM GILBERT
The Yeomen of the Guard, 1888

Owner of the King's Head Tavern, journalist and social commentator, Ned Ward recorded his impressions of London in a "Journal intended to expose the vanities and vices of the town." The London Spy, issued in monthly installments beginning in 1698, includes this description of his visit to the Royal Menagerie — one of the Tower's most exotic features.

I had oftentimes in the country heard wonderful tales from higglers, hawkers, carriers, drovers, and such-like hobbady-bobbodies, of several four-footed barbarian kings, with many of their ravenous subjects, who had for divers years been kept close prisoners in Her Majesty's palace and prison, the Tower of London....

The sundry reports of these amazing objects, together with many other enticing rarities, to be visited at a small expense within the ancient battlements of this renown'd citadel (which I had received from the magnifying mouths of some boobily bumpkins who had stolen so much time from their wagons and hay-carts as to be spectators of these surprising curiosities) had begot in me an earnest desire of beholding these foreign monsters, and domestic engines of destruction, with crowns, sceptres, and many other pompous knick-knacks worth any great man's coveting who prefers grandeur before ease, and riches before safety. So, having prevailed with my friend to concur with my proposal, we determined to steer towards this stately magazine, and to spend a little time in viewing the martial furniture of that famous garrison which statesmen dread and common people admire....

When we came upon Tower Hill, the first object that more particularly affected us was that emblem of destruction, the scaffold, from whence greatness, when too late, has oft beheld the happiness and security of lower stations; reflecting with a deep concern on their sudden prosperity, and the restless ambition that had brought 'em to that fate which the contentment, under a moderate fortune and a private life, might have happily prevented. For he that sits too high in the favour of his prince is liable to be deliver'd up, upon public disorders, as a sacrifice to appease the fury of the people; and he that labours for a popular esteem is always look'd upon by his prince to be a dangerous subject; so that (according to Phoebus's caution to his son Phaeton), 'tis safest to steer the course of our lives in a middle station....

Accordingly we went in, where the yard smelt as frowzily as a dove-house, or a dog-kennel. In their separate apartments were four of their stern affrighting catships, one with a whelp presented to his late Majesty, of which the dam was as fond as an old maid, when married, is of her first child; one couchant, another dormant, a third passant guardant, a fourth, very fierce, was rampant (being a lioness), and was so angry when we spoke to her, she put out her paw to me, which was tipt with such ill-favour'd sort of pruning-hooks, that rather than she should have taken me by the hand I would have chosen to have taken Old Nick by his cloven foot, and should have thought myself in less danger.

One of the keeper's servants, whilst he was showing us his unruly prisoners, entertain'd us with a couple of remarkable stories, which, because the tragedy of the one will render an escape in the other story the more providential, I shall proceed to give the reader.

Some years since, a maidservant to the keeper, and a bold spirited wench, took pleasure, now and then, to help feed the lions, and imprudently believing the gratitude of the beasts would not suffer them to hurt her, she would venture sometimes, tho' with extraordinary caution, to be a little more familiar with them than she ought to be. At last, either carelessly or presumptuously, she ventur'd too near their dens, and one of the lions catch'd hold of her arm, and tore it quite off the shoulder, after a most lamentable manner, before anybody could come to her assistance, killing her with a grip, before he would loose her from his talons, till she was made a miserable object of her own folly, the lion's fury and the world's pity.

This story was succeeded by another, wherein was shown a miraculous preservation of himself. "Tis our custom," says he, "when we clean the lions' dens, to drive 'em down over night thro' a trap-door, into a lower conveniency, in order to rise early in the morning and refresh their day-apartments, by clearing away their filth and nastiness. Having thro' mistake, and not forgetfulness, left one of the trap doors unbolted, which I thought I had carefully secured, I came down in the morning, before daylight, with my candle and lanthorn fasten'd before me to a button, with my implements in my hands to dispatch my business, as was usual; and going carelessly into one of the dens, a lion had returned thro' the trap-door, and lay crouched in a corner, with his head towards me. The sudden surprise of this terrible sight brought me under such dreadful apprehensions of the danger I was in that I stood fix'd like a statue, without the power of motion, with my eyes steadfastly upon the lion, and his likewise upon me. I expected nothing but to be torn to pieces every moment, and was fearful to attempt one step back, lest my endeavour to shun him might have made him the more eager to have hasten'd my destruction.

"At last he rous'd himself, as I thought to have made a breakfast of me; yet, by the assistance of Providence, I had the presence of mind to keep steady in my posture. He mov'd towards me without expressing in his countenance either greediness or anger, but on the contrary he wag'd his tail, signifying nothing but friendship in his fawning behaviour. And after he had stared me a little in the face, he rais'd himself upon his two hindmost feet and laying his two paws upon my shoulders without hurting me, fell to licking my face, as a further instance of his gratitude for my feeding him, as I afterwards conjectur'd, though then I expected every minute he would have strip'd my skin over my ears, as a poulterer does a rabbit, and have crack'd my head between his teeth as a monkey does a small-nut.

The Bishops are Sent to the Tower by Watter.

"His tongue was so very rough that with the few favourite kisses he gave me, it made my cheeks almost as raw as a pork grisken, which I was very glad to take in good part. . . . And when he had thus saluted me, and given me his sort of welcome to his den, he return'd to his place, and laid him down, doing me no further damage. This unexpected deliverance occasion'd me to take courage so that I slunk by degrees, till I recovered the trap-door, thro' which I jumped and pluck'd it after me; thus happily, thro' an especial Providence, I escaped the fury of so dangerous a creature". . . .

The next ill-favour'd creatures that were presented to our sight were a couple of pretty looking hell-cats, call'd a tiger, and a cat-a-mountain [panther], whose fierce penetrating eyes pierc'd thro' my belly to the sad griping of my guts, as if they would have kill'd at a distance with their looks.

In another apartment or ward, for the conveniency of drawing a penny more out of the pocket of a spectator, are plac'd the following animals: first a leopard, who is grown as cunning as a cross Bedlamite that loves not to be look'd at. The next creatures were three hawk-nosed gentlemen call'd eagles, one black, another in second mourning, a third with a bald pate, as if he had been pulling a crow [quarreling] with his two comrades, and like unmerciful enemies they had peck'd all the feathers off his crown. Next to these were a couple of outlandish owls, whose mouths lay under their beaks like an old citizen's under his nose after he has rotted out his teeth with eating custard at the Lord Mayor's feasts. These owls, besides eyes as big as the glasses of a convex-lamp, had each of them long ears that grew like horns, under which they look'd as venerably grave as two aged aldermen.

NED WARD
The London Spy, 1703

To the delight of visiting tourists, a number of mischievous ravens nest at the Tower. Under the special care of a Raven Master, they are fed a daily diet of raw meat paid for out of a special fund set aside by Parliament. If the ravens were to leave the Tower, according to an ancient tradition, the fortress and England itself would topple. The obdurate winged hero of this story clearly has no intention of leaving.

He was perched on the iron rail which spaces out the spot where the scaffold was erected on Tower Green in the bad old days, when I first made the startling discovery that he possessed the gift of speech.

He was one of the oldest and most sinister-looking of the four ravens which roam at will in the great space within the precincts of the Tower of London faced by the ancient Norman keep, and flanked by the Lieutenant's Lodging and the Chapel of St. Peter in Chains. After having piloted thither innumerable country cousins and American visitors, and saved from shame Londoners who had admitted in my hearing to never having seen the Tower, the existing thrills of the historic spot had somewhat staled for me when I discovered this new thrill, the raven with the gift of speech.

He looked old enough to have been present when the English headsman brought his ax down on the neck of the innocent Lady Jane Grey, or when the swordsman, brought from Calais, jerked the guilty head of Nan Boleyn from her fair shoulders — and wicked enough to have thoroughly enjoyed the spectacle!

He was plainly an old, old, very old bird. One wing was damaged, and the feathers protruded untidily. He had hopped in a lopsided fashion to his favorite perch (I was convinced that it was his favorite perch) and sat eying me coldly. I wondered what his exact age might be. Ravens are said to be rivals of Methuselah.

"If you could speak," I said, addressing him, meditatively, "you might tell me something worth hearing."

And at that moment a strange thing happened. A strange and an eerie thing. A passing beef-eater, as the warders of the Tower are quaintly called, caught sight of the bird and, pausing, called out to it. He called out, "Hullo!" And he called several times. At about the fourth or fifth call the ancient bird lifted a leg and shifted on its perch. Then it closed its eyes, covering them with a kind of film that added indescribably to its expression of all-knowing wickedness. For a moment it appeared to be in travail; it opened its beak to its widest extent, as though to void itself of something in its crop that had not agreed with it; then — it answered the salutation:

"Hul..lo!"

It was a hoarse, far-away, sepulchral cry. The sound of a salutation which might have been consigned to the ether centuries ago — an echo that might well have come from the dungeons in the White Tower, preferably "Little Ease."

"Hul..lo!"

The warder smiled at me and passed on his way. Ordinarily I would have detained him and asked some questions, for the Tower beef-eater is always ready to impart information, but on this occasion I was red-hot on a new stunt. I had discovered that one of the Tower ravens could talk. Who could want to speak to a beef-eater after that?

The bird remained on his perch. He closed his beak and opened, or rather cleared, his eyes, and regarded me with some return of the interest that I was taking in him. He was plainly open to be interviewed.

I began with the beef-eater gambit.

"Hullo," I said.

He eyed me suspiciously and vouchsafed no response.

I tried again, coming to the point this time with the question on the tip of my tongue.

"How old are you?" I asked. "How *old?*"

My Lord Chancellor in the Tower.

His immemorial years might have made him hard of hearing. He shifted on his perch, dipped and stretched forward his neck, rather as though he were making it ready for the headsman's ax (he really was a horrid bird), then closed his eye in the same nasty manner as before — a wink was nothing to it for knowingness — and made answer, in a deep, muffled tone:

"Old."

It was terse and indefinite. Laconic, one might say. But the tone in which the single word was delivered gave it a positively uncanny significance. It suggested that the evil, half-closed eye might have witnessed the influx of unwilling Jews into the dungeon where King John held them until they satisfied his tax-collecting propensities. This bird was part and parcel of the bad old days.

I grew hot and cold with excitement.

"How old?" I asked, boldly. "Three — four — hundred years?"

Whereat he became coy, like a maiden lady faced with the same question, and twisting his neck, tucked a bit of fluff into his torn wing. He was eying me cautiously and expectantly. I felt encouraged to persevere. I thought of all the things which he might have witnessed in the days we had left behind.

He was facing the old state prison in the Beauchamp Tower where Queen Elizabeth shut up the Earl of Arundel for the crime of having a wife, and a religion at variance with her own. Did the prisoner, looking out of his window, see a raven hopping about on the site of the scaffold which he so narrowly escaped? Surely his little dog, the one which followed the Lieutenant when he paid a visit to Father Robert Southwell in his dungeon, was not responsible for the damaged wing? Hardly, for the poet-saint gave the little dog his blessing. The encounter would certainly not have been on the homeward journey. It would be interesting to find out which was the dungeon which held the rarest singer, after Shakespeare, of Elizabethan times; but although I did my musing out loud, the bird did not come to my assistance.

At the recently made entrance to the vaults of the White Tower a warder was keeping at bay lawless groups of visitors who were seeking to enter by what the authorities have elected shall be the exit from the dungeons now shown to the public.

"Other times, other manners," I remarked. The bird made an audience and I was indulging an Emersonian mood. "In the old days I imagine it was not necessary to employ a warder to keep people out of the dungeons. Times have considerably improved."

The crowd was heading for the Wakefield Tower, where the crown jewels are kept. There would be almost as big a squeeze in the big, circular chamber as in the days when 600 prisoners were thrust into it after the battle of Wakefield, during the Wars of the Roses. The bird would hardly remember that circumstance, though he might know something about Guy Fawkes — he was probably hatched out by that date. But every warder can tell tales about Guy Fawkes; one would think that no one else had ever played with gunpowder. When I visited the Tower some years ago with a permit enabling me to enter the dungeons by the unorthodox way (I recall the privilege with pride) the dungeon called "Little Ease" had still got its door — it had not yet been made into a passage between the torture chamber and the Jews' dungeon — and my guide had shown me the marks made by the feet of the unhappy inmate, unable to stand upright or to lie at full length in the diabolically contrived cell. He had mentioned Guy Fawkes as a famous occupant of "Little Ease" but had nothing to say anent Father Edmund Campion, S.J., who was taken from "Little Ease," the place of confinement for infamous criminals, into the presence of Queen Elizabeth, who proceeded to offer him a bishopric if he would conform to the state religion. Campion declined the offer and returned to "Little Ease," which has thus its bishop-designate to counteract its gunpowder plotter, only no custodian appears to make use of the fact.

"By the way," I said to the raven, "what became of that door? I wonder what they did with it when they removed it?"

He blinked at me, silently. I interpreted the blink as: "Any warder could tell you that. Why ask me?" Which was true enough.

"It must have been just before the war," I calculated. "The Tower was closed during the war, of course."

The bird gave me a sharp glance. His colleagues were near by, fraternizing with some of the human species who were feeding them with assorted dainties, which appeared to be the normal mode of approach to a Tower raven. He eyed the note-book in my hand — I always carry one at the Tower — and the expression in his eye became cruel and sinister. I recognized that I was speaking to a bird of prey. He hopped along his perch, nearer to the site of the executioner's block, and sat with his head turned toward the barracks erected alongside the Church of St. Peter in Chains.

I followed his gaze, past the other ravens pecking up their largesse, to the great, modern, grey building which usually I make a point of ignoring, as any antiquarian would. It recalled to my mind the fact that the Tower had been closed to the public during the war for the very obvious reason that it was required for military uses. Internment, and other purposes. The Tower of London had come to life during the war. There had been a grim story told of the enemy's spies shot at daybreak, over yonder.

The raven was sharpening his beak on the rail surrounding the ancient place of execution. There was something horridly suggestive in the action.

I glanced back at the rude walls of the old keep which houses the suits of armor worn by men who fought the gentlemanly battles of the much criticized days of old. I thought of poison gas, and other methods of warfare, and the days which we had lived through, the raven and I, for in any case he must have been a pre-war bird.

"But it will never occur again," I said. "We have got our League of Nations, and disarmament is well on its way. There will never be another war. Nevermore will such a thing be permitted."

He closed his eyes and opened his beak. But there it ended. He might have followed in the footsteps of Edgar Poe's raven, but the wisdom of the ages was in his shabby pose, and whatever the traditions of talking ravens might be, he was not going to commit himself.

ENID DINNIS
Quoth the Raven, 1931

"BASKETBALL AND BEEFEATERS"

The grim aspects of the Tower's long history seem incompatible with the popular American sport of basketball. Yet in the twentieth century, an enterprising young American student arranged just such an interlude at the monument.

One season, during the middle nineteen-fifties, I was a member of the basketball team at Cambridge University.

During the Christmas vacation, I spent a fortnight in London, riding the high buses — once, inevitably, to the Tower. What American youth does not yearn to see the Tower of London? It is to poisoning, hanging, beheading, regicide, and torture what Yankee Stadium is to baseball. . . .

Standing there beside that block [where Anne Boleyn among others was beheaded] on an overcast December morning, I happened to see that my feet were straddling a white line painted on the asphalt of the parade ground that adjoins Waterloo Barracks, one of the substructures within the walls. Our guide, a Yeoman Warder, or Beefeater, in medieval costume, was probably saying that the barracks were built in the middle of the nineteenth century and are one of the youngest of the Tower's substructures . . . I was not listening to him. The white line made a large rectangle in the middle of the parade ground. There was a circle in the center and at each end the startling outlines of basketball foul lanes.

"Any questions?" the guide asked.

"Who plays basketball here?" I said.

There must have been thirty people on the tour, and they all turned around to look at me. Some of them laughed nervously. I thought for a moment that I had imagined the court. But then the guide explained that the Tower is garrisoned by Her Majesty's Royal Fusiliers. They stay in shape by playing basketball during non-visiting hours.

When I returned to Cambridge, I instantly got hold of the secretary of the basketball club and urged him to write to the Royal Fusiliers and set up a match. He said I was daft; but he wrote the letter. The Royal Fusiliers responded at once. They had a building in which they played their matches, but they were delighted that Cambridge University would like to play them in their Tower.

It was the last match of our season, toward the end of the Lent term. A Beefeater led us through a gate in the Tower walls. He was excited about the game, talking animatedly as he walked, kicking ravens out of his path and praising the sharpshooting skills of the Royal Fusiliers. . . . When the lorry finally came [carrying the baskets and backboards], we were out on the parade ground dressed and ready, the Royal Fusiliers in dark uniforms, Cambridge in pale Cambridge blue. . . .

The lorry backed up to the foot of one foul lane and stopped. Two soldiers got on the tailgate. They shoved the heavy steel mounting out the back end and tilted it upward until its twin poles were secured in casings embedded in the asphalt. There at last stood the phenomenon I had been waiting to see, a basketball hoop, net, and backboard rising up in the very center of the Tower of London. In moments, we would be sending long one-handed shots arcing past the high battlements, adding a wild footnote to the history of the game. Meanwhile, the lorry driver prepared to move off to the other end of the court. After a great gnashing of gears, he started up with a violent jolt — and surged backward rather than forward, smashing into the support poles of the erected basket and snapping them off at the ground. The soldiers didn't even bother to set up the other basket. It was just jolly bad luck, that was all. There was a lot of swearing on the part of the Fusiliers, and the lorry driver had to take considerable mockery. For my part, I would have settled for an improvised half-court game there in the Tower, but that apparently did not cross the minds of our hosts, who had never completely understood why we wanted to play in the Tower in the first place.

We all climbed into the lorry and were driven to a sports hall near Tower Hill. . . . We would have been uncharitable to admit our disappointment, but the ultimate score of the game was probably an indirect expression of it — Cambridge 95, Royal Fusiliers 42. It was the worst beheading in the history of the Tower, inside or outside the walls.

JOHN MCPHEE
Basketball and Beefeaters, 1963

The late D of M beheaded on Tower Hill 15 July 1685

REFERENCE

Chronology of English History

Entries in boldface refer to the Tower.

1066	William the Conqueror invades England
1078	**Construction begun on White Tower; Geoffrey de Mandeville appointed first Tower Constable**
c. 1080	**Chapel of St. John consecrated**
1085	Domesday Book census taken
1091	**Storm-damaged White Tower repaired**
1100	**Flambard, first prisoner, escapes**
1140	**First used as royal residence**
1170	Thomas à Becket murdered
1215	John grants Magna Carta
1216–72	**Reign of Henry III, major builder**
c. 1221	**Wakefield Tower built**
1241	**White Tower whitewashed; Becket's "ghost" damages St. Thomas's Tower**
1264	**Royal Menagerie founded; Simon de Montfort briefly captures Tower**
1297	**King Baliol of Scotland imprisoned**
c. 1300	**Beauchamp Tower built**
1308	**Knights Templar imprisoned**
c. 1322	**Ceremony of the Keys begun**
1337	Outbreak of Hundred Years' War
1346	**King David Bruce of Scotland held**
1348–49	Black Death decimates population
1356–60	**John II of France held for ransom**
1381	**Mob storms Tower in Peasants' Revolt**
1399	**Richard II deposed and imprisoned**
1415	**Dukes of Orleans and Bourbon imprisoned after battle of Agincourt**
1431	Joan of Arc burned at stake by English
1450	**Cade's rebels attack Tower**
1455–85	Wars of the Roses
1471	**Henry VI mysteriously dies**
c. 1483	**York princes murdered**
1485	Henry Tudor defeats Richard III at Bosworth Field
1487	Star Chamber court established
1512	**St. Peter ad Vincula burned down**

1520	**Rebuilding of St. Peter ad Vincula completed**
1530	**Queen's House built**
1532	**St. Thomas's Tower remodeled**
1534	Act of Supremacy declares Henry VIII head of Church of England
1535	**Sir Thomas More and Bishop John Fisher beheaded**
1536	**Anne Boleyn beheaded**
1540	**Thomas Cromwell beheaded**
1541	**Margaret, Countess of Salisbury, executed**
1542	**Catherine Howard beheaded**
1554	**Lady Jane Grey beheaded**
1555–58	Bloody Mary persecutes Protestants
1563	Elizabeth I completes establishment of Anglican Church
1577–80	Sir Francis Drake sails around world
1587	Mary Queen of Scots executed
1588	Spanish Armada defeated
1597	**Father John Gerard escapes**
1601	**Earl of Essex beheaded**
1605	**Guy Fawkes and Gunpowder Plot conspirators tortured**
1607	Founding of Jamestown colony
1613	**Sir Thomas Overbury poisoned**
1618	**Sir Walter Ralegh executed**
1625	Accession of Charles I
1642–46	Civil War
1648	Second Civil War
1649	Charles I beheaded at Whitehall
1649–60	**Crown jewels sold or melted down during Commonwealth period**
1653	Oliver Cromwell named Lord Protector
1658	**Royalists attempt to seize Tower**
1660	**Regicides imprisoned following Restoration of Charles II; last use of Tower as royal residence**
1665	Great Plague strikes London

1666	**Great Fire threatens Tower**
1669	**William Penn imprisoned**
1671	**Attempted theft of crown jewels**
1674	**Skeletons believed to be those of York princes found**
1678	**Popish Plot conspirators imprisoned**
1679	Habeas Corpus Act passed
1679	**Samuel Pepys imprisoned**
1683	**Rye House plotters imprisoned**
1685	**Duke of Monmouth executed**
1688	Glorious Revolution of William and Mary
1689	**Judge Jeffreys dies in Tower**
1694	**Christopher Wren supervises repairs**
1707	Parliamentary union with Scotland
1715	**Jacobite rebels imprisoned**
1716	**Lord Nithsdale escapes**
1717	**Middle Tower refaced**
1745	**More Jacobite rebels imprisoned**
1747	**Lord Lovat beheaded**
1756–63	Seven Years' War with France
1760	**Earl Ferrers imprisoned for murder**
1764	**John Wilkes imprisoned**
1775–83	War for American Independence
1780	**Anti-Catholic Gordon rioters storm Tower; last executions held at Tower Hill**
1798	**Attempted theft at Royal Mint**
1801	Parliamentary union with Ireland
1810	**Royal Mint removed from Tower**
1815	Duke of Wellington defeats Napoleon at Waterloo
1820	**Cato Street conspirators imprisoned**
1826	**Wellington named Tower Constable**
1833	Slavery abolished in colonies
1834	**Royal Menagerie removed**
1841	**Fire damages Tower structures**
1843	**Victoria orders moat drained**

c. 1844	**Salvin undertakes major repairs**
1845	**Waterloo Barracks built**
1857	**Chapel of St. John restored**
1868–94	Ministries of Disraeli and Gladstone
1870	**Crown jewels moved to Wakefield Tower**
1875	Suez Canal purchased
1876	**St. Peter ad Vincula restored; Lanthorn Tower rebuilt**
1885	**Irish Fenians plant bombs at Tower**
1898–99	**Ancient Roman wall excavated**
1901	Death of Victoria
1914	**War declared on Germany; Carl Lody, German naval officer, shot as spy**
1915	**Seven German spies shot**
1916	**Roger Casement imprisoned**
1919	Treaty of Versailles
1924	First Labour Government
1936	Edward VIII abdicates
1939	War declared on Germany
1939	**Tower closed; crown jewels removed**
1940–45	Ministry of Winston Churchill
1940	**Bombs damage Tower**
1941	**German Deputy Fuhrer Rudolf Hess imprisoned; Josef Jakobs shot as spy**
1944	**Bombs explode near Tower**
1945	**Tower floodlit as symbol of peace**
1946	**Tower reopened to public**
1946–49	Nationalization program enacted
1948	**Crown jewels returned**
1953	Coronation of Elizabeth II
1956	Withdrawal from Suez
1957	**Remains of Henry III's water gate uncovered**
1963	**Sound and light shows held**
1966	**Modern entrance completed**
1967	**New Jewel House opened**
1970	**Memorial to Sir Thomas More unveiled**

Guide to the Tower of London

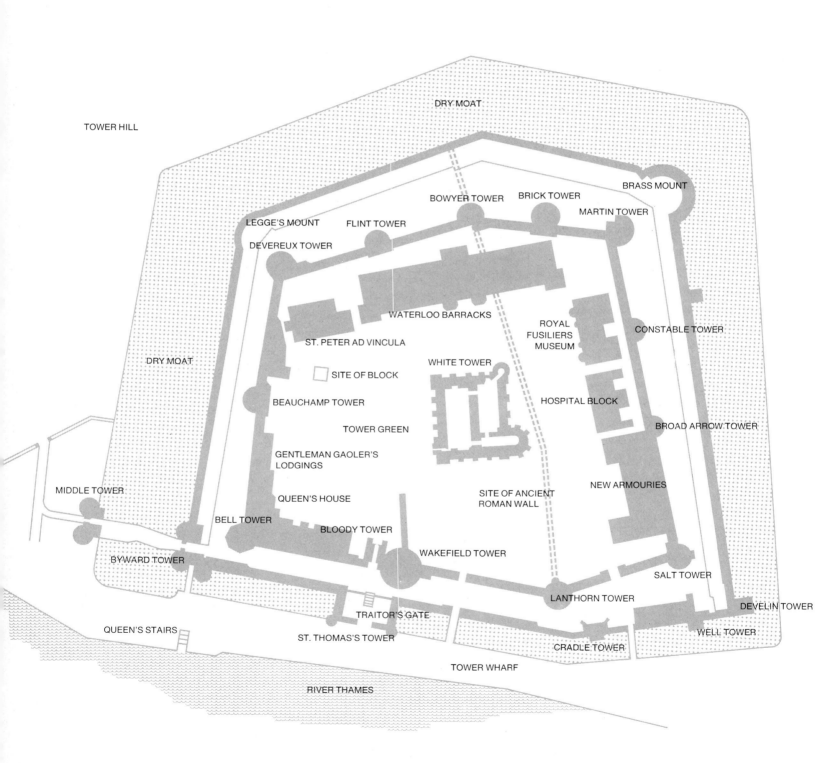

TOWER HILL

DRY MOAT

BRASS MOUNT

BOWYER TOWER

BRICK TOWER

MARTIN TOWER

LEGGE'S MOUNT

FLINT TOWER

DEVEREUX TOWER

WATERLOO BARRACKS

ROYAL FUSILIERS MUSEUM

CONSTABLE TOWER

ST. PETER AD VINCULA

DRY MOAT

WHITE TOWER

☐ SITE OF BLOCK

BEAUCHAMP TOWER

HOSPITAL BLOCK

TOWER GREEN

BROAD ARROW TOWER

GENTLEMAN GAOLER'S LODGINGS

NEW ARMOURIES

MIDDLE TOWER

QUEEN'S HOUSE

SITE OF ANCIENT ROMAN WALL

BELL TOWER

BLOODY TOWER

BYWARD TOWER

WAKEFIELD TOWER

SALT TOWER

LANTHORN TOWER

DEVELIN TOWER

TRAITOR'S GATE

QUEEN'S STAIRS

ST. THOMAS'S TOWER

WELL TOWER

CRADLE TOWER

TOWER WHARF

RIVER THAMES

Awesome symbol of England's national heritage, the Tower of London is actually a massive fortress complex of twenty towers that covers an eighteen-acre site on the River Thames at the southeast reach of modern London.

In the center and dominating the site is the *White Tower,* the oldest structure in the complex. In 1078 William the Conqueror ordered its construction — the final link in a chain of castles built around London by the Normans to defend the city against attacks by their newly conquered Anglo-Saxon subjects. Gundulf, Bishop of Rochester, was probably the architect who effected William's plan, although construction and repairs continued throughout the reigns of the Conqueror's two sons, William Rufus and Henry I.

Soaring to a height of 90 feet and measuring 118 feet by 107 feet, the White Tower or Keep was designed as an impregnable fortress; it housed a garrison as well as the royal court. Its walls, of blond limestone from Caen in Normandy and coarse ragstone from nearby Kent, are supported by massive buttresses and vary in thickness from fifteen feet at the base to eleven feet at the top. Slender turrets top its four corners. Although it appears square, the Keep is actually irregular; only one corner forms a right angle. The building is bisected by a wall that runs north and south through the entire structure, and its eastern half is divided by another wall that forms the Chapel of St. John. Arched windows were added in the eighteenth century by the famed English architect Christopher Wren.

The name White Tower dates from the thirteenth century, when Henry III, who was more responsible for the present appearance of the Tower complex than any other single monarch, ordered the four-story exterior and the royal apartments whitewashed.

In 1100 the White Tower was host to the first of many hundreds of state prisoners — the agile Bishop Rannulf Flambard, who slid down a rope from his top-floor cell and swam across the moat to freedom. It was stormed by a mob during the Peasants' Revolt of 1381 and, ironically, was the abdication site, eighteen years later, of Richard II — who had saved the Tower from destruction during the same uprising.

By the sixteenth century the Keep was supplanted by other towers as the principal prison within the Tower complex, and during the seventeenth century it assumed a more peaceful and lasting role as the Royal Armouries — England's oldest museum. Its rooms still house magnificent collections of armor, bows, lances, swords, small arms, decorated cannon, and other instruments of war.

The austere *Chapel of St. John,* on the second floor of the White Tower, is the best-preserved and one of the most beautiful Romanesque chapels in England. Built of Caen stone, it dates from about 1080, although many structural repairs were made later, particularly in the seventeenth century. The clerestory windows look down on a chamber measuring 55½ feet by 31 feet. Spanning the nave and apse is the only perfect barrel vault in England. Twelve heavy, round pillars support a triforium, once set aside for use by the female members of the court. The carved capitals of the columns provide the stark chapel's only decorative relief.

The famed order of the Knights of the Bath has long been associated with the Chapel of St. John. In an elaborate ceremony, the honored knights bathed in huge tubs in the Sword Room, kept an all-night vigil over their armor in the chapel, and were anointed by the king-to-be on the following morning, the day of his coronation.

Below the chapel is the dreaded *Dungeon of the Little Ease.* Smallest of the three dungeons in the White Tower, it measures only four feet square and kept a prisoner constantly on his feet. Its oak doors blocked all light and ventilation. Among the many prisoners tortured in Little Ease were members of the Knights Templar in the thirteenth century; Guy Fawkes, a leader of the Gunpowder Plot in the seventeenth century; and the noted eighteenth-century Jacobite rebel Lord Lovat. Lovat, in 1747, was the last man beheaded in England. Instruments of torture — the rack, thumbscrews, gauntlets, and the Spanish collar — are displayed in the dungeon.

Over the centuries, the Conqueror's successors — particularly Henry III (1216–72) and Edward I (1272–1307) — improved the fortress's defenses. They built towers, walls, and gateways of many architectural styles, until the Tower complex assumed its familiar form.

The present fortress consists of three lines of defense. First is the wall of the outer ward, which is broken by six towers and two bastions and abuts the Thames wharf to the south. Second, surrounding the outer ward is a one-hundred-foot-wide moat that was drained by Queen Victoria in 1843 and filled to a height of fifteen feet with oyster shells. Third is the forty-foot-high wall of the inner ward and its thirteen towers, which ring a large area that includes the White Tower and many other structures.

The modern entrance to the Tower is over a stone causeway, which was built by Edward I in 1278. It once crossed a small outer moat and led to a semicircular structure called the Lion Tower. This building housed the Royal Menagerie from the time of Henry III until 1834; it was later torn down.

Entering the Tower grounds from the west, a visitor encounters the *Middle Tower* first. Begun by Edward I, this structure was rebuilt in the early eighteenth century: its walls were refaced, huge windows were set into its east and west fronts, and the coats-of-arms of the Hanoverian kings were carved over its wide archway.

A stone bridge leads from the Middle Tower across the moat to the *Byward Tower,* the gate house of the outer ward. This battlement was built by Edward I; Richard II added an upper story; and a timber superstructure, including a gallery, was constructed in the early sixteenth century. Until 1810 the Royal Mint was housed in a nearby building.

Directly opposite the Byward Tower to the east is the *Bell Tower,* built into the inner wall. Probably planned by Richard I, it was completed in the thirteenth century. Many prominent prisoners were held there, including Sir Thomas More, Bishop John Fisher, the Duke of Monmouth, and the future Queen Elizabeth I.

As a prisoner, Elizabeth dined in the picturesque *Queen's House* in the inner ward, just east of the Bell Tower. The timber-framed house with window boxes and iron balconies was built in 1530 and was known as the Lieutenant's Lodgings until 1880. Originally it was a large hall, but alterations were later made to add the historic council chamber, scene of such significant events as the interrogation of the Gunpowder Plot conspirators in 1605; the imprisonment of William Penn (who later founded the American colony of Pennsylvania) in 1669; and the incarceration of Nazi leader Rudolf Hess, who deserted Germany during World War II. In a small room in the north wing on the upper floor, Anne Boleyn was imprisoned before her execution.

Adjoining the Queen's House is the *Gentleman Gaoler's Lodgings.* From a window, Lady Jane Grey saw her husband taken to his execution on Tower Hill, overlooking the Tower complex.

While Elizabeth was a prisoner in the Bell Tower she was permitted to walk along the battlements that joined her prison to the *Beauchamp Tower* to the north. Named for Thomas Beauchamp, a political prisoner of Richard II, the Beauchamp Tower is due west of the White Tower. A semicircular three-story structure that projects eighteen feet beyond the face of the wall, the Beauchamp Tower was built by Edward I. It was the favorite prison of the Tudor kings, and its walls are rich with inscriptions carved by many victims.

East of the Beauchamp Tower in the inner ward is *Tower Green,* where several famous prisoners met their deaths. Queen Victoria erected a small paved plot to mark the site of the wooden scaffolds on which at least seven persons died: Lord Hastings, Anne Boleyn, the Countess of Salisbury, Catherine Howard, Lady Rochford, Lady Jane Grey, and Robert Devereux, Earl of Essex.

With many others who died at the Tower, all of the victims executed on Tower Green were buried nearby in the *Chapel of St. Peter ad Vincula,* a superb example of Norman architecture. The chapel was consecrated during the reign of Henry I, rebuilt in the thirteenth century, burned down in 1512, again rebuilt in 1520, and restored in 1876.

North of the chapel is the huge Neo-Gothic *Waterloo Barracks,* built in 1845 on the site of the Great Storehouse, which burned to the ground in 1841. It now houses England's crown jewels. To the east are two other structures: the *Royal Fusiliers Museum,* housing trophies and relics of the City of London Regiment and a large collection of silver and china; and the *Small Armouries,* a red brick building dating from the late seventeenth century that complements the White Tower's collection of armor.

Five towers are built into the northern inner wall: the two-story *Devereux Tower* on the northwest, which takes its name from Robert Devereux, second Earl of Essex, and was probably built by Henry III; *Flint Tower,* built by Henry III and rebuilt in 1796, formerly containing a dungeon known as Little Hell; *Bowyer Tower,* once the quarters of the king's bowmaker, which dates in part from the reign of Henry III; *Brick Tower,* built by Henry III and completely restored in the nineteenth century; and *Martin Tower,* also built by Henry III.

Martin Tower has a rather varied history. The crown jewels and royal finery were moved there from the White Tower in the mid-seventeenth century, and shortly thereafter Colonel Blood made a daring but unsuccessful attempt to steal them. Eleven spies were shot near Martin Tower during World War I, and bombs damaged the building in World War II.

North of Martin Tower are two bastions at the corners of the outer wall — *Legge's Mount* and *Brass Mount,* built by Henry VIII for mounted cannon.

South of Martin Tower and also on the inner wall are: *Constable Tower,* built by Henry III and completely rebuilt in the nineteenth century; *Broad Arrow Tower,* also built by Henry III and containing sixteenth-century inscriptions made by Roman Catholic prisoners, and *Salt Tower,* at the southeast corner. Formerly called Julius Caesar's Tower because it was said the ancient Romans had built a fortress on the site, Salt Tower contains the second largest number of prisoners' inscriptions after the Beauchamp Tower. Many Jesuits were held there, including Father John Gerard, who survived torture in the White Tower and escaped.

Built into the southern inner wall are *Lanthorn Tower* and *Wakefield Tower.* Part of Henry III's palace, Lanthorn Tower burned in 1788, but was rebuilt to its original plan in 1876 by the architect Anthony Salvin. In the inner ward, directly opposite, is the site of an ancient Roman wall. Wakefield Tower, also built by Henry III, was once known as Hall or Record Tower because it housed the nation's official records. Its present name honors William de Wakefield, King's Clerk to Edward III. On the second floor is a chamber where Henry VI reputedly was murdered while praying. In the nineteenth century, Gothic windows were added, the battlements were restored, and the walls were refaced.

Until 1967 Wakefield Tower was the home of the crown jewels of England. Oliver Cromwell sold or melted down most of the treasure during the Commonwealth period (1649–60), when the monarchy was briefly abolished. As much as possible was recovered when the monarchy was restored, and duplicates were made of pieces destroyed. This fabulous collection, which includes jewel-encrusted crowns, orbs, swords of state, royal scepters, royal plate, gold spurs, and the coronation ampulla and spoon, is displayed behind sturdy plate glass. During World War II the crown jewels were moved to a hiding place that is still a state secret and were returned to the Tower in 1948.

Next to Wakefield Tower is the monument's most infamous structure — the *Bloody Tower,* which once served as the gateway to the inner ward. The lowest level was built by Henry III. Above it, a tower was constructed by Henry Yevele, the fourteenth century's leading architect. Its portcullis, or grated, sliding door, weighs two tons and is the only one in England in working condition. Before the Duke of Wellington, a Constable of the Tower, installed a windlass and pulleys in 1848, thirty men were required to raise and lower it.

Unlike most of the towers in the fortress, the Bloody Tower is square-shaped. Once known as the Garden Tower because it overlooked the constable's garden, its present name dates from at least the sixteenth century and derives from the probable murder there of the York princes. It is said that their bodies were first buried under Wakefield Tower, then reburied beneath a staircase in the White Tower. In 1674 workmen dis-

covered two skeletons reputed to be theirs, which were reinterred at Westminster Abbey. Among the many other famous prisoners held in the Bloody Tower were Sir Walter Ralegh, the popular courtier; Sir Thomas Overbury, who was slowly poisoned to death; Archbishop Cranmer, who was burned at the stake for heresy; the infamous Judge Jeffreys; and Arthur Thistlewood, leader of the Cato Street conspiracy of 1820.

The southern edge of the Tower of London faces directly on the Thames. Set into this outer ragstone bulwark constructed by Edward I are four towers: the *Develin Tower,* on the southeast; the *Well Tower,* with a vault dating from the reign of Henry III; *Cradle Tower,* a fourteenth-century structure with a water gate that once opened directly onto the river; and *St. Thomas's Tower.* The last, built by Henry III, was restored in 1512, and again in 1866 by Salvin, who also constructed the enclosed bridge linking it to Wakefield Tower, directly opposite in the inner wall. In a vaulted chamber of the tower is a small oratory dedicated to Thomas à Becket, the obdurate prelate martyred by Henry II's followers in 1170.

Beneath this dark, forbidding tower is *Traitor's Gate,* probably built by Henry III. Today the gate is approximately fifty feet from the Thames, but its stairs once led directly into the water. Charged with treason and brought to the Tower by barge, Sir Thomas More, Anne Boleyn, Elizabeth I, Catherine Howard, the Duke of Monmouth, and countless other less famous prisoners passed beneath the heavy iron and wood gate into the Tower and heard it shut behind them with a finality that frequently spelled death.

The Royal Houses of England

(Edward III, grandfather of the first Lancastrian king, Henry IV, was a direct descendant of William the Conqueror, whose three Norman and eight Plantagenet successors ruled England for more than three centuries.)

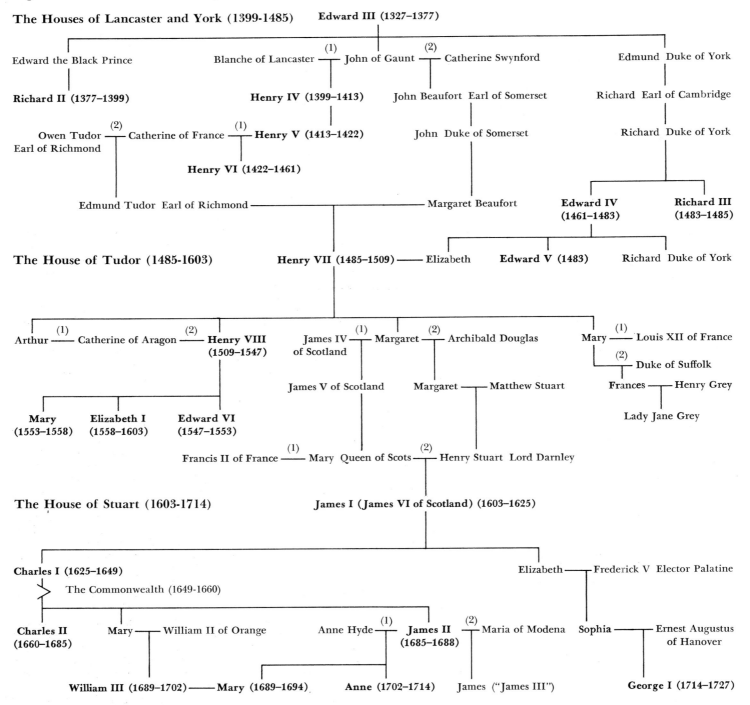

The Houses of Lancaster and York (1399-1485) — Edward III (1327–1377)

Edward the Black Prince — Blanche of Lancaster (1) John of Gaunt (2) Catherine Swynford — Edmund Duke of York

Richard II (1377–1399) — Henry IV (1399–1413) — John Beaufort Earl of Somerset — Richard Earl of Cambridge

Owen Tudor Earl of Richmond (2) — Catherine of France (1) Henry V (1413–1422) — John Duke of Somerset — Richard Duke of York

Henry VI (1422–1461)

Edmund Tudor Earl of Richmond — Margaret Beaufort — Edward IV (1461–1483) — Richard III (1483–1485)

The House of Tudor (1485-1603) — Henry VII (1485–1509) — Elizabeth — Edward V (1483) — Richard Duke of York

Arthur (1) — Catherine of Aragon (2) Henry VIII (1509–1547) — James IV of Scotland (1) Margaret (2) Archibald Douglas — Mary (1) Louis XII of France / (2) Duke of Suffolk

James V of Scotland — Margaret — Matthew Stuart — Frances — Henry Grey

Mary (1553–1558) — Elizabeth I (1558–1603) — Edward VI (1547–1553) — Lady Jane Grey

Francis II of France (1) — Mary Queen of Scots (2) Henry Stuart Lord Darnley

The House of Stuart (1603-1714) — James I (James VI of Scotland) (1603–1625)

Charles I (1625–1649) — The Commonwealth (1649-1660) — Elizabeth — Frederick V Elector Palatine

Charles II (1660–1685) — Mary — William II of Orange — Anne Hyde (1) James II (1685–1688) (2) Maria of Modena — Sophia — Ernest Augustus of Hanover

William III (1689–1702) — Mary (1689–1694) — Anne (1702–1714) — James ("James III") — George I (1714–1727)

(George I, founder of the House of Hanover, was Queen Victoria's great-great-great-grandfather. The same number of generations—five—separates Victoria from Prince Charles, heir-apparent to the English throne.)

Selected Bibliography

Bowled, John. *Henry VIII: A Biography*. Boston: Little, Brown and Co., 1964.

Costain, Thomas Bertram. *The Three Edwards*. New York: Doubleday & Co., Inc., 1958.

Denny, Norman and Filmer-Sankey, Josephine. *The Bayeux Tapestry. The Story of the Norman Conquest: 1066*. New York: Atheneum Publishers, 1966.

Elton, G. R. *England Under the Tudors*. New York: Barnes & Noble, Inc., 1955.

Fraser, Antonia. *Mary Queen of Scots*. New York: Delacorte Press, 1969.

Galbraith, V. H. *The Making of the Domesday Book*. New York: Oxford University Press, Inc., 1961.

Gardiner, S. R. *Oliver Cromwell*. London: Longmans, Green Ltd., 1925.

Garvin, Katharine, ed. *The Great Tudors*. London: Eyre & Spottiswoode Ltd., 1956.

Hanson, Michael. *2000 Years of London*. London: Country Life Ltd., 1967.

Hearsey, John E. N. *The Tower: 880 Years of English History*. London: Macgibbon & Kee Ltd., 1960.

Hibbert, Christopher. *London: A Biography of a City*. New York: William Morrow & Co., Inc., 1970.

Hill, Christopher. *The Century of Revolution, 1603-1714*. Edinburgh: Thomas Nelson and Sons, Ltd., 1961.

Kenyon, J. P. *The Stuarts*. London: B. T. Batsford Ltd., 1958.

Maurois, André. *An Illustrated History of England*. New York: Viking Press, Inc., 1964.

Minney, R. J. *The Tower of London*. Englewood Cliffs: Prentice-Hall, Inc., 1970.

Neale, J. E. *Queen Elizabeth I*. New York: St. Martin's Press, Inc., 1959.

Nicoll, Allardyce. *The Elizabethans*. New York: Cambridge University Press, 1957.

Plumb, J. H. *England in the Eighteenth Century*. Harmondsworth: Penguin Books Ltd., 1950.

Price, Mary Roper. *A Portrait of Britain in the Middle Ages, 1066-1485*. Oxford: Clarendon Press, 1951.

Slocombe, George Edward. *William the Conqueror*. London: Hutchinson Ltd., 1959.

Smith, Lacey Baldwin. *The Horizon Book of the Elizabethan World*. New York: American Heritage Publishing Co., Inc., 1967.

Trevelyan, G. M. *Illustrated History of England*. London: Longmans, Green Ltd., 1956.

Wallace, Willard Moshe. *Sir Walter Raleigh*. Princeton: Princeton University Press, 1959.

Acknowledgments and Picture Credits

The Editors make grateful acknowledgment for the use of excerpted material from the following works:

Anne of the Thousand Days by Maxwell Anderson. Copyright 1948 by Maxwell Anderson. The excerpt appearing on pages 139-41 is reproduced by permission of William Morrow and Company, Inc.

"Basketball and Beefeaters" by John McPhee. Copyright 1963 by The New Yorker Magazine, Inc. The excerpt appearing on pages 159-60 is reproduced by permission of *The New Yorker*.

The London Spy by Ned Ward. Copyright 1955 by The Folio Society Ltd. The excerpt appearing on pages 154-56 is reproduced by permission of The Folio Society Ltd.

"Quoth the Raven" by Enid Dinnis. Copyright 1931 by *Commonweal*. The excerpt appearing on pages 156-59 is reproduced by permission of *Commonweal*.

The Editors would like to express their particular appreciation to Russell Ash in London for his invaluable assistance in obtaining pictorial material, and to Anthony Howarth in London for creative photography. The title or description of each picture appears after the page number (boldface), followed by its location. Photographic credits appear in parentheses.

ENDPAPERS Aquatint of the Tower of London from the Thames by William Daniell, 1804. London Museum HALF TITLE Symbol designed by Jay J. Smith Studio FRONTISPIECE Close helmet embossed with lion's mask and damascened with gold, French or Italian, *c.* 1540-50. The Armouries, Tower of London (Anthony Howarth) 10 Majolica dish made *c.* 1600 for Queen Elizabeth I. London Museum 12 Pole-axe, German, 1490. The Armouries (Anthony Howarth)

CHAPTER I 17 top, Flagship of William the Conqueror; bottom, The battle of Hastings; Both from the Bayeux tapestry, Canterbury, A.D. 1070-80. Musée de la Tapisserie, Bayeux (Michael Holford) 19 Manuscript illumination of William the Conqueror presenting fiefs to his nephew, Alain Le Roux, Count of Brittany, from *Registrum Honoris Richmondiae,* 13th century. British Museum, Ms. Cotton Faustina B, vii. fol 72v 20 Castle at Rochester Cathedral (A. F. Kersting) 21 The White Tower (Ministry of Public Buildings & Works: Crown Copyright) 22-23 Detail showing the Tower of London, from Anthony van den Wyngaerde's view of London, *c.* 1543-50. Bodleian Library, Oxford 24-25 The Chapel of St. John (Nino Mascardi, Mondadori) 26-27 Engraving of the Tower of London by Hayward and Gascoyne, 1597. British Museum, London 28 Manuscript illumination of a royal feast, from Jehan de Grise's *The Romance of Alexander,* Flanders, 1339-44. Bodleian Library, Oxford, Ms. Bodley 264, fol 72v 29 left, Manuscript illumination of two courtiers playing chess, from Jehan de Grise's *The Romance of Alexander*, Flanders, 1339-44. Bodleian Library, Oxford, Ms. Bodley 264, fol 121v. **29** right, Manuscript illumination of a hunting scene, from a Book of Hours belonging to Engelbert of Nassau, Flanders, 1485-90. Bodleian Library, Oxford, Ms. Douce 219-20, fol 56

CHAPTER II **32** Manuscript illumination of Richard II being imprisoned in the Tower, September 3, 1399. British Museum, Ms. Harleian 4380, fol 181v. **34** Manuscript illumination of the murder of the Archbishop of Canterbury in the Tower during the Peasants' Revolt of 1381, from Jean Froissart's *Chroniques de France et d'Angleterre*, 1460-80. British Museum, Ms. Royal 18, E. i., fol 172 **35** Manuscript illumination of Richard II confronting the people at Mile End and the Lord Mayor of London killing Wat Tyler, from Jean Froissart's *Chroniques de France et d'Angleterre*, 1460-80. British Museum, Ms. Royal 18, E. i., fol 175 **38-39** Manuscript illumination of Richard II abdicating to Henry of Lancaster in the council chamber of the White Tower on September 29, 1399. British Museum, Ms. Harleian 4380, fol 184v **41** Manuscript illumination of the Court of the King's Bench during the reign of Henry VI, from the *Whaddon Folio*, c. 1460. By courtesy of the Masters of the Bench of the Inner Temple, Ms. 440 **43** Engraving of King Richard III, from Henry Holland's *Baziliwlogia*, 1618. Spencer Collection, New York Public Library **44** Staircase in the White Tower (Anthony Howarth)

CHAPTER III **48** Manuscript illumination of the duke in the Tower after the battle of Agincourt, from a book of poems of Charles, Duke of Orléans, c. 1487. British Museum, Ms. Royal 16, F.i.i., fol 73 **52** Sketch of Sir Thomas More and his family by Hans Holbein. The Kupferstichkabinett, Basel **53** Detail showing London Bridge from C. J. Visscher's map of London, 1616. British Museum **54** Drawing of Anne Boleyn by Hans Holbein. Weston Park, Courtauld Institute **55** Portrait of Jane Seymour by Hans Holbein. Kunsthistorisches Museum, Vienna **56-57** Tower Green (Anthony Howarth) **60** Engraving of Henry VIII by Cornelis Matys, 1544. British Museum **61** top left, Portrait of Catherine Howard by Hans Holbein. The Toledo Museum of Art, Toledo, Ohio. Gift of E. D. Libbey **61** top right, Portrait of Thomas Cromwell by Hans Holbein. The Frick Collection **61** bottom, Portrait of Henry Howard, Earl of Surrey, by William Scrots, 1550. By permission of the Duke of Norfolk **63** Block and axe (Anthony Howarth) **64** Painting of antipapal allegory, 1548. The National Portrait Gallery, London

CHAPTER IV **68-69** Engraving of the coronation procession of Edward VI, from the *Vetusta Monumenta*. Society of Antiquaries, London **71** Inscription on a wall in the Beauchamp Tower (Anthony Howarth) **72** Portrait of Lady Jane Grey by Master John, c. 1545. The National Portrait Gallery, London **73** View from a window in the Gentleman Gaoler's Lodgings (Anthony Howarth) **74-75** Illustrations of the beheading of Lady Jane Grey by George Cruikshank, from W. Harrison Ainsworth's *The Tower of London*, 1840. Astor, Lenox & Tilden Foundations, Rare Book Division, New York Public Library **76** Manuscript illumination of Prince Griffin falling from the Tower, from Matthew Paris's *Historia Minor*. British Museum, Ms. Royal 14, C. viii., fol 136 **77** Traitor's Gate (Anthony Howarth) **78-79** Pen and ink drawing of the coronation procession of Elizabeth I, 1559. British Museum, Ms. Egerton 3320, fol 5 **80** Portrait of Elizabeth I in her coronation robes, by an unknown artist, 1559. Lord Brooke **81** The Elizabeth Salt, 1572. British Crown Copyright. Reproduced by permission of the Controller of Her Britannic Majesty's Stationery Office **82-83** Woodcut of Elizabeth I at a picnic, from George Turberville's *The Noble Arte of Venerie or Hunting*, 1575. British Museum **84** Title page from Sir Walter Ralegh's *The Historie of the World*, 1634 edition. Astor, Lenox & Tilden Foundations, Rare Book Division, New York Public Library

CHAPTER V **88** German print of Guido Fawkes and the Gunpowder plotters, 1606. British Museum **88-89** The council chamber in the Queen's House (Anthony Howarth) **91** Woodcut of the racking of Cuthbert Simson in the Tower, from John Foxe's *History of the Actes and Monuments of the Church*, 1610 edition. British Museum **92** Portrait of Sir Thomas Overbury by Marcus Gheeraerts. Bodleian Library, Oxford **93** The altar of St. Peter ad Vincula (Anthony Howarth) **94** Engraving of the execution of the Earl of Strafford by Wenceslaus Hollar, 1641. Greater London Council **96** Portrait of Samuel Pepys by J. Hayls, 1666. The National Portrait Gallery, London **97** Dutch print of the 1666 London fire by Marcus Willemsz Doornick. British Museum **98** Queen of Hearts playing card showing Popish plotter Everard in Tower, 1678. British Museum, Pack E. 58 **100** Wash drawing of troops and cannon at Tower, anonymous, 17th century. British Museum **102-3** Colored aquatint of the Tower from the River Thames by J. Gendall and D. Havell, 1819. British Museum

CHAPTER VI **106** Colored engraving of a lion, tiger, and tigress fighting in the Tower menagerie by S. Maunder, December 3, 1830. The Guildhall, London **107** Admission ticket to the ceremony of washing the lions, April 1, 1857. British Museum **109** Suit of armor made for Henry VIII at Greenwich, 1535-40. The Armouries (Anthony Howarth) **111** Close helmet made for William Somerset at Greenwich, 1570-80. The Armouries (Anthony Howarth) **110-11** Manuscript illumination of Henry VIII jousting before Catherine of Aragon, from the *Westminster Tournament Roll,* 16th century. College of Arms, London **112** Spiked club with three pistol barrels in the head, known as "Henry VIII's Walking Staff." The Armouries (Anthony Howarth) **114** top, The Imperial Crown of State; bottom, The Ampulla and Spoon. Both, British Crown Copyright. Reproduced by permission of the Controller of Her Britannic Majesty's Stationery Office **115** The Sceptre with the Cross. British Crown Copyright. Reproduced by permission of the Controller of Her Britannic Majesty's Stationery Office **117** Proclamation issued by Charles II for the arrest of "Captain" Blood, 1667. British Museum **118** Portrait of Henry Wriothesley and detail from portrait, by John de Critz, 1603. The Duke of Buccleuch and Queensberry, K.T., G.C.V.O. **121** The State Salt, gift from the city of Exeter. British Crown Copyright. Reproduced by permission of the Controller of Her Britannic Majesty's Stationery Office

CHAPTER VII **124** Colored engraving of *The Beheading of the Rebel Lords on Great Tower Hill,* August 18, 1746. London Museum **127** Engraving of Simon Fraser, Lord Lovat, by William Hogarth, 1747. Metropolitan Museum of Art **128** top, Colored lithograph of the Brick Tower after the 1841 fire, by William Oliver. Greater London Council **128** bottom, Colored engraving of the destruction of the Small Armouries, 1841, by Ackerman. The Guildhall, London **130-31** Colored lithograph of the Tower and Mint from Great Tower Hill, by Thomas Shotter Boys, 1842. The Guildhall, London **133** Print of the Yeoman Warders, 1888. Mansell Collection **135** The Ceremony of the Keys (Ministry of Public Buildings & Works: Crown Copyright) **136** Sword and rapier, 1620. The Armouries (Anthony Howarth)

THE TOWER OF LONDON IN LITERATURE **138-60** Ten 17th-century playing cards depicting the Tower during the Popish Plot, the Monmouth Rebellion, and the Essex Rebellion. British Museum, Packs E.56, E.62, E.63, E.191

REFERENCE **164** Map of Tower of London by Jay J. Smith Studio

Index